the good cook®

BOOK OF DAYS 2006

First published in the USA in 2005 by Bookspan
15 East 26th Street, 4th & 5th Floors
New York, NY 10010

Copyright © Bookspan 2005
Text copyright © Duncan Baird Publishers 2005

Created and designed by Bookspan and
Duncan Baird Publishers

Text and recipes: Julia Charles, Joan Duncan Oliver
Editor: Rebecca Miles
Designer: Gail Jones
Designer (food photography): Sailesh Patel
Commissioned photography including cover: William Lingwood
Stylists: Lucy McKelvie (food) and Helen Trent

Color reproduction by Color & Print Gallery Sdn Bhd, Malaysia
Manufactured in China

Acknowledgments
Illustrations by Susy Pilgrim Waters (Lilla Rogers Studio) and
Gianpaolo Pagni (Marlena Agency, Inc.)

Susy Pilgrim Waters: Dec 26–1 Jan; Jan 9–15; Jan 23–29; Feb 6–12; Feb 20–26; Mar 6–12; Mar
20–26; April 3–9; April 17–23; May 1–7; May 15–21; May 29–4 June; June 12–18; June 26–2 July;
July 10–16; July 24–30; Aug 7–13; Aug 21–27; Sept 4–10; Sept 18–24; Oct 2–8; Oct 16–22; Oct
30–5 Nov; Nov 13–19; Nov 27–3 Dec; Dec 11–17; Dec 25–31.

Gianpaolo Pagni: Jan 2–8; Jan 16–22; Jan 30–5 Feb; Feb 13–19; Feb 27–5 Mar; Mar 13–19; Mar
27–2 April; April 10–16; April 24–30; May 8–14; May 22–28; June 5–11; June 19–25; July 3–9;
July 17–23; July 31–6 Aug; Aug 14–20; Aug 28–3 Sept; Sept 11–17; Sept 25–1 Oct; Oct 9–15; Oct
23–29; Nov 6–12; Nov 20–26; Dec 4–10; Dec 18–24.

The publishers would like to thank Andrew Wood/The Interior Archive, London for permission to
reproduce their photograph on the Welcome page.

Publisher's Note

2005

JANUARY
M	TU	W	TH	F	SA	SU
					1	2
3	4	5	6	7	8	9
10	11	12	13	14	15	16
17	18	19	20	21	22	23
24	25	26	27	28	29	30
31						

FEBRUARY
M	TU	W	TH	F	SA	SU
	1	2	3	4	5	6
7	8	9	10	11	12	13
14	15	16	17	18	19	20
21	22	23	24	25	26	27
28						

MARCH
M	TU	W	TH	F	SA	SU
	1	2	3	4	5	6
7	8	9	10	11	12	13
14	15	16	17	18	19	20
21	22	23	24	25	26	27
28	29	30	31			

APRIL
M	TU	W	TH	F	SA	SU
				1	2	3
4	5	6	7	8	9	10
11	12	13	14	15	16	17
18	19	20	21	22	23	24
25	26	27	28	29	30	

MAY
M	TU	W	TH	F	SA	SU
						1
2	3	4	5	6	7	8
9	10	11	12	13	14	15
16	17	18	19	20	21	22
23	24	25	26	27	28	29
30	31					

JUNE
M	TU	W	TH	F	SA	SU
		1	2	3	4	5
6	7	8	9	10	11	12
13	14	15	16	17	18	19
20	21	22	23	24	25	26
27	28	29	30			

JULY
M	TU	W	TH	F	SA	SU
				1	2	3
4	5	6	7	8	9	10
11	12	13	14	15	16	17
18	19	20	21	22	23	24
25	26	27	28	29	30	31

AUGUST
M	TU	W	TH	F	SA	SU
1	2	3	4	5	6	7
8	9	10	11	12	13	14
15	16	17	18	19	20	21
22	23	24	25	26	27	28
29	30	31				

SEPTEMBER
M	TU	W	TH	F	SA	SU
			1	2	3	4
5	6	7	8	9	10	11
12	13	14	15	16	17	18
19	20	21	22	23	24	25
26	27	28	29	30		

OCTOBER
M	TU	W	TH	F	SA	SU
					1	2
3	4	5	6	7	8	9
10	11	12	13	14	15	16
17	18	19	20	21	22	23
24	25	26	27	28	29	30
31						

NOVEMBER
M	TU	W	TH	F	SA	SU
	1	2	3	4	5	6
7	8	9	10	11	12	13
14	15	16	17	18	19	20
21	22	23	24	25	26	27
28	29	30				

DECEMBER
M	TU	W	TH	F	SA	SU
			1	2	3	4
5	6	7	8	9	10	11
12	13	14	15	16	17	18
19	20	21	22	23	24	25
26	27	28	29	30	31	

2006

JANUARY
M	TU	W	TH	F	SA	SU
						1
2	3	4	5	6	7	8
9	10	11	12	13	14	15
16	17	18	19	20	21	22
23	24	25	26	27	28	29
30	31					

FEBRUARY
M	TU	W	TH	F	SA	SU
		1	2	3	4	5
6	7	8	9	10	11	12
13	14	15	16	17	18	19
20	21	22	23	24	25	26
27	28					

MARCH
M	TU	W	TH	F	SA	SU
		1	2	3	4	5
6	7	8	9	10	11	12
13	14	15	16	17	18	19
20	21	22	23	24	25	26
27	28	29	30	31		

APRIL
M	TU	W	TH	F	SA	SU
					1	2
3	4	5	6	7	8	9
10	11	12	13	14	15	16
17	18	19	20	21	22	23
24	25	26	27	28	29	30

MAY
M	TU	W	TH	F	SA	SU
1	2	3	4	5	6	7
8	9	10	11	12	13	14
15	16	17	18	19	20	21
22	23	24	25	26	27	28
29	30	31				

JUNE
M	TU	W	TH	F	SA	SU
			1	2	3	4
5	6	7	8	9	10	11
12	13	14	15	16	17	18
19	20	21	22	23	24	25
26	27	28	29	30		

JULY
M	TU	W	TH	F	SA	SU
					1	2
3	4	5	6	7	8	9
10	11	12	13	14	15	16
17	18	19	20	21	22	23
24	25	26	27	28	29	30
31						

AUGUST
M	TU	W	TH	F	SA	SU
	1	2	3	4	5	6
7	8	9	10	11	12	13
14	15	16	17	18	19	20
21	22	23	24	25	26	27
28	29	30	31			

SEPTEMBER
M	TU	W	TH	F	SA	SU
				1	2	3
4	5	6	7	8	9	10
11	12	13	14	15	16	17
18	19	20	21	22	23	24
25	26	27	28	29	30	

OCTOBER
M	TU	W	TH	F	SA	SU
						1
2	3	4	5	6	7	8
9	10	11	12	13	14	15
16	17	18	19	20	21	22
23	24	25	26	27	28	29
30	31					

NOVEMBER
M	TU	W	TH	F	SA	SU
		1	2	3	4	5
6	7	8	9	10	11	12
13	14	15	16	17	18	19
20	21	22	23	24	25	26
27	28	29	30			

DECEMBER
M	TU	W	TH	F	SA	SU
				1	2	3
4	5	6	7	8	9	10
11	12	13	14	15	16	17
18	19	20	21	22	23	24
25	26	27	28	29	30	31

2007

JANUARY
M	TU	W	TH	F	SA	SU
1	2	3	4	5	6	7
8	9	10	11	12	13	14
15	16	17	18	19	20	21
22	23	24	25	26	27	28
29	30	31				

FEBRUARY
M	TU	W	TH	F	SA	SU
			1	2	3	4
5	6	7	8	9	10	11
12	13	14	15	16	17	18
19	20	21	22	23	24	25
26	27	28				

MARCH
M	TU	W	TH	F	SA	SU
			1	2	3	4
5	6	7	8	9	10	11
12	13	14	15	16	17	18
19	20	21	22	23	24	25
26	27	28	29	30	31	

APRIL
M	TU	W	TH	F	SA	SU
						1
2	3	4	5	6	7	8
9	10	11	12	13	14	15
16	17	18	19	20	21	22
23	24	25	26	27	28	29
30						

MAY
M	TU	W	TH	F	SA	SU
	1	2	3	4	5	6
7	8	9	10	11	12	13
14	15	16	17	18	19	20
21	22	23	24	25	26	27
28	29	30	31			

JUNE
M	TU	W	TH	F	SA	SU
				1	2	3
4	5	6	7	8	9	10
11	12	13	14	15	16	17
18	19	20	21	22	23	24
25	26	27	28	29	30	

JULY
M	TU	W	TH	F	SA	SU
						1
2	3	4	5	6	7	8
9	10	11	12	13	14	15
16	17	18	19	20	21	22
23	24	25	26	27	28	29
30	31					

AUGUST
M	TU	W	TH	F	SA	SU
		1	2	3	4	5
6	7	8	9	10	11	12
13	14	15	16	17	18	19
20	21	22	23	24	25	26
27	28	29	30	31		

SEPTEMBER
M	TU	W	TH	F	SA	SU
					1	2
3	4	5	6	7	8	9
10	11	12	13	14	15	16
17	18	19	20	21	22	23
24	25	26	27	28	29	30

OCTOBER
M	TU	W	TH	F	SA	SU
1	2	3	4	5	6	7
8	9	10	11	12	13	14
15	16	17	18	19	20	21
22	23	24	25	26	27	28
29	30	31				

NOVEMBER
M	TU	W	TH	F	SA	SU
			1	2	3	4
5	6	7	8	9	10	11
12	13	14	15	16	17	18
19	20	21	22	23	24	25
26	27	28	29	30		

DECEMBER
M	TU	W	TH	F	SA	SU
					1	2
3	4	5	6	7	8	9
10	11	12	13	14	15	16
17	18	19	20	21	22	23
24	25	26	27	28	29	30
31						

WELCOME TO 2006

I'm delighted to present *The Good Cook Book of Days 2006*—our first. If you're as busy as I am, you're always looking for something to help you stay organized and make life easier. Finally, I think I've found it.

The Good Cook Book of Days is more than just an appointment book. It's two resources in one. There's plenty of room to schedule daily activities, but this is also a comprehensive cooking guide, packed with recipes, kitchen lore, and useful information on preparing food. I plan to keep my copy on the kitchen counter so I can jot down menus and grocery lists throughout the week, and refer to the recipes and tips while cooking. I'm also giving a copy to everyone I know who cares about cooking great meals but, like me, is pressed for time.

Each month there's a featured recipe, made with seasonal ingredients, that would be perfect to serve on a holiday or special occasion. Dozens more recipes and tips appear on the weekly pages. As an added bonus, there are sections on table setting and serving cocktails.

The Good Cook Book of Days was great fun to compile, and I hope you'll enjoy using it as much as we enjoyed putting it together. I look forward to your comments on what you find most helpful.

Patricia Adrian

Patricia Adrian
Editor-in-Chief, The Good Cook

Roasted Onion and Tomato Soup

WITH GREEN DUMPLINGS

Not everyone has an Italian grandmother to share her recipes. Fortunately, *cucina casalinga*, Italy's traditional home-style cooking, is accessible to us all. This is simple, hearty fare made from humble but high-quality ingredients—the best of the garden, market, and larder. A tasty tomato-and-onion soup with herbed goat-cheese dumplings is the sort of robust yet sophisticated dish that works equally well for family suppers or informal entertaining. Just add a green salad, crusty bread, and a Chianti classico.

INGREDIENTS *Makes 4–6 servings*

2 carrots, unpeeled

3 Spanish onions, trimmed and halved, skins left on

2 lbs plum (Italian) tomatoes, skins left on

4 garlic cloves, peeled

1½ cups soft goat cheese

¼ cup fresh breadcrumbs

salt and black pepper

1 large egg, beaten

1 tbsp each chives, flat-leaf parsley, and fresh basil, finely chopped

1½ pts vegetable or chicken stock

METHOD

1 Preheat oven to 400°F. Cut the carrots in half lengthwise, and place on a heavy baking sheet with the garlic cloves, onion halves (cut side down), and tomatoes (standing core end down). Bake for 40 minutes.

2 To make the dumplings, put the goat cheese in a bowl and mash well with a fork. Mix in the breadcrumbs and herbs. Season to taste. Mix in the beaten egg. Take a teaspoonful of mixture at a time and mold into small dumplings.

3 When the vegetables are cooked, allow them to cool slightly and then remove their skins. Place them, and any juices, into the jug of a blender and top up with the stock. Blend, and pour the soup through a sieve into a saucepan.

4 Heat the soup until simmering, season, and then add the dumplings. Poach for 3–4 minutes, until they're firm. Serve immediately.

"So long as there's water, there's tea."

MONDAY 26 Boxing Day (Canada), Kwanzaa begins

AM

PM

TUESDAY 27

AM

PM

WEDNESDAY 28

AM

PM

THURSDAY 29

AM

PM

FRIDAY 30

AM

PM

QUICK TIP

To ensure a longer refrigerator life for mushrooms, remove them from any plastic packaging, put them in a paper bag or wrap in paper towels, then place them in a plastic bag with holes punched for air circulation before putting them in the refrigerator.

	Su	M	T	W	Th	F	S	Su	M	T	W	Th	F	S	Su	M	T	W	Th	F	S	Su	M	T	W	Th	F	S	Su	M	T	W	Th	F	S
DECEMBER			1	2	3	4	5	6	7	8	9	10	11	12	13	14	15	16	17	18	19	20	21	22	23	24	25	26	27	28	29	30	31	
JANUARY	1	2	3	4	5	6	7	8	9	10	11	12	13	14	15	16	17	18	19	20	21	22	23	24	25	26	27	28	29	30	31				
FEBRUARY		1	2	3	4	5	6	7	8	9	10	11	12	13	14	15	16	17	18	19	20	21	22	23	24	25	26	27	28						

FOOD IN A FLASH

RIGATONI WITH CREAMY BACON AND MUSHROOM SAUCE

(serves 2)

Cook sufficient rigatoni pasta for 2 people in a large pot of boiling salted water. Meanwhile, heat 1 tablespoon olive oil in a large skillet, add 1 small leek, sliced, 2 slices bacon, coarsely chopped, and 1 clove garlic, crushed. Add 1 large zucchini, sliced, and ½ cup button mushrooms, also sliced. Cook, stirring, until the zucchini is just tender and the bacon is crisp. Stir in 1 tablespoon Dijon mustard, ½ cup light sour cream, and ½ cup milk and cook, stirring, until heated through. Toss the sauce through the cooked, drained pasta and serve immediately.

SATURDAY 31   New Year's Eve

AM   PM

SUNDAY 1   New Year's Day

AM   PM

PANTRY RUNNING LOW ON

"Happiness: a good bank account, a good cook, and a good digestion."
Jean Jacques Rousseau (1712–1778)

MONDAY 2

AM

PM

TUESDAY 3

AM

PM

WEDNESDAY 4

AM

PM

THURSDAY 5

AM

PM

FRIDAY 6

AM

PM

QUICK TIP

It's simple and inexpensive to make your own crème fraîche. Just stir together 1 cup heavy cream and 1 tablespoon buttermilk. Let this stand at warm room temperature for 9 to 12 hours, then cover, and refrigerate.

	Su	M	T	W	Th	F	S	Su	M	T	W	Th	F	S	Su	M	T	W	Th	F	S	Su	M	T	W	Th	F	S	Su	M	T	W	Th	F	S
DECEMBER			1	2	3	4	5	6	7	8	9	10	11	12	13	14	15	16	17	18	19	20	21	22	23	24	25	26	27	28	29	30	31	
JANUARY	1	2	3	4	5	6	7	8	9	10	11	12	13	14	15	16	17	18	19	20	21	22	23	24	25	26	27	28	29	30	31				
FEBRUARY		1	2	3	4	5	6	7	8	9	10	11	12	13	14	15	16	17	18	19	20	21	22	23	24	25	26	27	28						

COOK'S PANTRY

HOT CHILI VINEGAR

This spicy vinegar is perfect for pepping up soups and sauces. Place 1 oz (about 8) dried chilies in a jar. Heat 2½ cups of red wine or sherry vinegar until just boiling, then pour over the dried chilies. Let the mixture cool, then cover tightly and leave for 2–3 weeks, shaking the jar occasionally. Strain the flavored vinegar into a clean bottle, making sure that the bottle is full to the top. Cover and store in a cool, dark place.

SATURDAY 7

AM

PM

SUNDAY 8

AM

PM

PANTRY RUNNING LOW ON

MONDAY 9

AM

PM

TUESDAY 10

AM

PM

WEDNESDAY 11

AM

PM

THURSDAY 12

AM

PM

FRIDAY 13

AM

PM

QUICK TIP

To peel onions easily and without tears, soak them in plenty of cold water for 20 to 30 minutes first. This toughens the skin, so it will pull off more easily, and the cold inhibits the gases that burn your eyes.

	Su	M	T	W	Th	F	S	Su	M	T	W	Th	F	S	Su	M	T	W	Th	F	S	Su	M	T	W	Th	F	S	Su	M	T	W	Th	F	S
DECEMBER						1	2	3	4	5	6	7	8	9	10	11	12	13	14	15	16	17	18	19	20	21	22	23	24	25	26	27	28	29	30	31
JANUARY	1	2	3	4	5	6	7	8	9	10	11	12	13	14	15	16	17	18	19	20	21	22	23	24	25	26	27	28	29	30	31
FEBRUARY		1	2	3	4	5	6	7	8	9	10	11	12	13	14	15	16	17	18	19	20	21	22	23	24	25	26	27	28

FOOD IN A FLASH

SPEEDY BEEF STROGANOFF

(serves 2)

Heat 1 tablespoon butter in a skillet. Add 1 white onion, chopped, and cook, stirring, until the onion softens. Add another tablespoon butter and, when melted, add 1 cup button mushrooms, sliced, and cook for a further 4–5 minutes. Stir in ½ teaspoon ground nutmeg and season to taste with salt and black pepper. Spoon into a bowl and set aside. Cut 12 oz lean beef fillet into strips and stir-fry in the hot skillet with 1 tablespoon olive oil until cooked. Return the mushroom mixture to the skillet, add 1 teaspoon Dijon mustard and ⅓ cup crème fraîche or heavy cream, and heat through. Sprinkle with paprika before serving with white rice.

SATURDAY 14

AM

PM

SUNDAY 15

AM

PM

PANTRY RUNNING LOW ON

"Part of the secret of success in life is to eat what you like and let the food fight it out inside."

Mark Twain (1835–1910)

MONDAY 16   Martin Luther King, Jr. Day

TUESDAY 17

WEDNESDAY 18

THURSDAY 19

FRIDAY 20

QUICK TIP

If you've made an unfrosted cake several hours ahead but want to serve it warm, place it on a sheet pan, lightly spritz the pan with water, cover with an aluminum foil tent, and reheat for a few minutes in a moderate oven.

	Su	M	T	W	Th	F	S	Su	M	T	W	Th	F	S	Su	M	T	W	Th	F	S	Su	M	T	W	Th	F	S	Su	M	T	W	Th	F	S
DECEMBER					1	2	3	4	5	6	7	8	9	10	11	12	13	14	15	16	17	18	19	20	21	22	23	24	25	26	27	28	29	30	31
JANUARY	1	2	3	4	5	6	7	8	9	10	11	12	13	14	15	16	17	18	19	20	21	22	23	24	25	26	27	28	29	30	31				
FEBRUARY		1	2	3	4	5	6	7	8	9	10	11	12	13	14	15	16	17	18	19	20	21	22	23	24	25	26	27	28						

COOK'S PANTRY

CANDIED PEEL

Choose thick-skinned oranges or lemons, and wash and dry them well. Finely peel the fruit and cut the peel into thin julienne strips. For each piece of fruit, combine 1 cup water with ½ cup sugar in a pan, and bring to a boil. Add the strips of peel, half-cover the pan, and simmer until the syrup has reduced by about three-quarters. Let cool. Sift confectioner's sugar in a thick layer over a baking sheet. Roll the peel in the sugar. Dry in a cool oven. Store the candied peel in a jar for up to 3 months.

SATURDAY 21

AM

PM

SUNDAY 22

AM

PM

PANTRY RUNNING LOW ON

JANUARY 23 – 29

MONDAY 23

AM

PM

TUESDAY 24

AM

PM

WEDNESDAY 25

AM

PM

THURSDAY 26

AM

PM

FRIDAY 27

AM

PM

QUICK TIP

To make clean-up super quick, spray your food processor's blade, disks, and bowl with a vegetable-oil spray before grating firm cheese or processing sticky mixtures—it will be a whole lot easier to get clean!

FOOD IN A FLASH

POTATO GNOCCHI WITH CREAMY BLUE CHEESE SAUCE

(serves 2)

Heat 1 cup heavy cream in a small, heavy-based saucepan until it starts to bubble. Reduce heat and let simmer. Add 2 tablespoons butter and let cook for 10 minutes. Meanwhile, in a large pot of boiling salted water, cook sufficient ready-made potato gnocchi to serve 2 people. Drain and return to the pan. Add 4 oz blue cheese (such as Roquefort or Gorgonzola) to the reduced cream and stir as it melts. Pour over the gnocchi and gently fold in. Season to taste with salt and black pepper and serve immediately with a tomato salad.

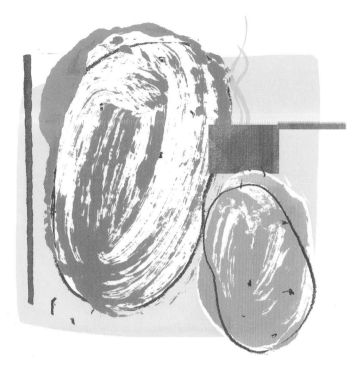

SATURDAY 28

AM

PM

SUNDAY 29   Chinese New Year (Year of the Dog)

AM

PM

PANTRY RUNNING LOW ON

Hot Chocolate Soufflé

WITH WHITE CHOCOLATE SAUCE AND RASPBERRIES

What would Valentine's Day be without chocolate? It was the legendary lover Casanova's elixir of seduction, and confectioners today still concoct no end of sweets to showcase its charms. But is chocolate really a love potion and mood-elevator, as claimed? While scientists debate its merits, we're free to draw our own conclusions. This soufflé with raspberries and white chocolate sauce certainly offers proof of chocolate's irresistible power.

INGREDIENTS *Makes 2–4 servings*

a pat of unsalted butter for greasing

⅓ cup superfine sugar, plus extra for sprinkling

5 oz bittersweet chocolate

3 large egg yolks

6 large egg whites

a pinch of salt

½ cup whipping cream

8 oz white chocolate, chopped

1 cup fresh raspberries

METHOD

1 Preheat oven to 375°F. Butter a single 5½-inch soufflé dish, or two 3-inch dishes, and sprinkle with sugar, knocking out the excess.

2 Break the bittersweet chocolate into pieces and melt in a bowl set over a saucepan of simmering water, stirring occasionally until smooth. Remove the bowl from the heat and stir in the egg yolks—the mixture will thicken.

3 Beat the egg whites with a pinch of salt in a large bowl until they just hold soft peaks. Add the sugar, beating in a little at a time; then, when it has all been added, beat until the whites hold stiff peaks. Stir 1 cup of this mixture into the chocolate mixture, then add this to remaining whites, folding gently.

4 Spoon into the prepared dish or dishes. Bake in the middle of the oven until puffed and crusted on top—15–25 minutes, depending on dish size.

5 Meanwhile, bring the cream to a simmer in a heavy saucepan. Remove from the heat. Add the white chocolate. Stir until melted, and add the raspberries. Pour over the soufflé once it has been served onto individual plates.

JANUARY 30 — 5 FEBRUARY

"Many's the long night I've dreamed of cheese — toasted, mostly..."

Robert Louis Stevenson (1850–1894)

MONDAY 30

TUESDAY 31

WEDNESDAY 1

THURSDAY 2   Groundhog Day

FRIDAY 3

QUICK TIP

For the flakiest pastry, freeze butter solid, then grate it with the grating disk of a food processor, or by hand, right into the flour. Add whatever liquid the recipe calls for, and finish making the dough as quickly as possible.

	Su	M	T	W	Th	F	S	Su	M	T	W	Th	F	S	Su	M	T	W	Th	F	S	Su	M	T	W	Th	F	S	Su	M	T	W	Th	F
JANUARY	1	2	3	4	5	6	7	8	9	10	11	12	13	14	15	16	17	18	19	20	21	22	23	24	25	26	27	28	29	30	31			
FEBRUARY	1	2	3	4	5	6	7	8	9	10	11	12	13	14	15	16	17	18	19	20	21	22	23	24	25	26	27	28						
MARCH	1	2	3	4	5	6	7	8	9	10	11	12	13	14	15	16	17	18	19	20	21	22	23	24	25	26	27	28	29	30	31			

COOK'S PANTRY

FLAVORED SUGARS

Wonderfully flavorful and fragrant, vanilla and cinnamon sugars are simple to make and can be used as an ingredient or decoration for baked goods, desserts, and beverages. To make, fill a jar with superfine sugar and press either a whole vanilla bean or 2 cinnamon sticks into the center. Seal and let infuse for 2–3 weeks. Alternatively, you can make a mixed spiced sugar in the same way, using a combination of whole spices such as cloves, cinnamon sticks, star anise, or cardamom pods.

SATURDAY 4

SUNDAY 5

PANTRY RUNNING LOW ON

FEBRUARY 6 – 12

"Worries go down better with soup."
Jewish proverb

MONDAY 6

AM

PM

TUESDAY 7

AM

PM

WEDNESDAY 8

AM

PM

THURSDAY 9

AM

PM

FRIDAY 10

AM

PM

QUICK TIP

To stop those little bits of chopped garlic from sticking to your fingers or your knife while you are working, simply dunk the clove in ice-cold water before skinning and slicing it.

	Su	M	T	W	Th	F	S	Su	M	T	W	Th	F	S	Su	M	T	W	Th	F	S	Su	M	T	W	Th	F	S	Su	M	T	W	Th	F
JANUARY	1	2	3	4	5	6	7	8	9	10	11	12	13	14	15	16	17	18	19	20	21	22	23	24	25	26	27	28	29	30	31			
FEBRUARY		1	2	3	4	5	6	7	8	9	10	11	12	13	14	15	16	17	18	19	20	21	22	23	24	25	26	27	28					
MARCH		1	2	3	4	5	6	7	8	9	10	11	12	13	14	15	16	17	18	19	20	21	22	23	24	25	26	27	28	29	30	31		

FOOD IN A FLASH

RED THAI-STYLE CURRIED PORK WITH BASIL
(serves 4)

Take 4 thin pork steaks and spread one side of each one with ½ teaspoon curry paste (preferably red Thai) and 1 teaspoon coconut cream. Fold in half, paste sides together, to seal. Heat 1 tablespoon peanut oil in a large skillet. Add the pork and fry until cooked through and browned on both sides. Remove from the skillet and keep warm. Add 2 tablespoons curry paste to the skillet and cook, stirring, until fragrant. Add ¾ cup chicken stock, and bring to a boil. Stir in 4 tablespoons coconut cream and ¼ cup shredded fresh basil until heated through. Spoon the sauce over the pork and serve with white rice.

SATURDAY 11

AM

PM

SUNDAY 12   Lincoln's Birthday

AM

PM

PANTRY RUNNING LOW ON

"Whatever will satisfy hunger is good food."
Chinese proverb

MONDAY 13

TUESDAY 14   Valentine's Day

WEDNESDAY 15

THURSDAY 16

FRIDAY 17

QUICK TIP

If you use only part of a batch of pie dough or puff pastry, just add a splash of vinegar to what you won't be using that day. Wrap the leftovers in foil or plastic wrap and place in the refrigerator. The vinegar will keep the dough white for up to a week.

	Su	M	T	W	Th	F	S	Su	M	T	W	Th	F	S	Su	M	T	W	Th	F	S	Su	M	T	W	Th	F	S	Su	M	T	W	Th	F
JANUARY	1	2	3	4	5	6	7	8	9	10	11	12	13	14	15	16	17	18	19	20	21	22	23	24	25	26	27	28	29	30	31
FEBRUARY		1	2	3	4	5	6	7	8	9	10	11	12	13	14	15	16	17	18	19	20	21	22	23	24	25	26	27	28
MARCH		1	2	3	4	5	6	7	8	9	10	11	12	13	14	15	16	17	18	19	20	21	22	23	24	25	26	27	28	29	30	31

COOK'S PANTRY

ITALIAN BLACK OLIVE PASTE

Known as *pasta di olive* in Italy, this versatile ingredient can be spread thinly over pizza bases, scraped onto toasted ciabatta, or added to a tomato pasta sauce. And a spoonful stirred into a vinaigrette makes a great salad dressing. Mix together 1 cup chopped, pitted black olives, 2 garlic cloves, chopped, 4 tablespoons chopped fresh parsley, 1 tablespoon chopped fresh thyme, and 5 tablespoons olive oil in a food processor. Season to taste with black pepper. Store in an airtight jar in the refrigerator and use within 2 weeks.

SATURDAY 18

SUNDAY 19

PANTRY RUNNING LOW ON

MONDAY 20   President's Day

TUESDAY 21

WEDNESDAY 22   George Washington's Birthday

THURSDAY 23

FRIDAY 24

QUICK TIP

Fresh basil and other fresh herbs hate to be chilled and will quickly become limp and blacken. Rather than refrigerating them, put the stems in a glass of water when you get home and keep the herbs in a cool place in your kitchen.

	Su	M	T	W	Th	F	S	Su	M	T	W	Th	F	S	Su	M	T	W	Th	F	S	Su	M	T	W	Th	F	S	Su	M	T	W	Th	F
JANUARY	1	2	3	4	5	6	7	8	9	10	11	12	13	14	15	16	17	18	19	20	21	22	23	24	25	26	27	28	29	30	31			
FEBRUARY		1	2	3	4	5	6	7	8	9	10	11	12	13	14	15	16	17	18	19	20	21	22	23	24	25	26	27	28					
MARCH		1	2	3	4	5	6	7	8	9	10	11	12	13	14	15	16	17	18	19	20	21	22	23	24	25	26	27	28	29	30	31		

FOOD IN A FLASH

SPEEDY CIABATTA PIZZAS
(serves 2)

Slice an Italian ciabatta loaf (or wide French stick) horizontally to give 2 flat bases. Broil these lightly until pale golden. Spread each with black olive paste (see recipe for February 13–19). Cut 2 slices of prosciutto ham into strips and lay some on each base (or use strips of canned or bottled red pimientos for a vegetarian option). Thinly slice a ball of mozzarella cheese and cover each "pizza" with it. Drizzle with olive oil and season to taste with salt and black pepper. Cook under a hot broiler until the cheese softens. Serve immediately with a green salad.

SATURDAY 25

AM

PM

SUNDAY 26

AM

PM

PANTRY RUNNING LOW ON

Lamb Casserole

WITH PEARL BARLEY AND RED WINE

St. Patrick's Day is the one time of year when everybody's got a bit o' the Irish in them. What to serve the crowd? Try this variation on a traditional Irish lamb stew. Adding red wine and tomatoes gives it a French twist. The boiled potatoes—a staple ingredient of the original—can be mashed and served as a side dish instead. What hasn't changed is the ease of one-pot cooking. Just assemble the ingredients and pop the pot in the oven for two hours. That leaves plenty of time to raise a glass to good health and good friends.

INGREDIENTS *Makes 4 servings*

2 tbsp olive oil
8 lean lamb shanks (loin chops if preferred)
2 medium onions
3 garlic cloves, crushed
4 medium carrots, chopped

½ cup pearl barley, rinsed and drained
1 cup dry red wine
1 cup beef stock
1 13-oz can chopped tomatoes

¼ cup tomato paste
1 tbsp fresh thyme, finely chopped
salt and black pepper

METHOD

1 Preheat oven to 350°F. Heat the oil in a medium flame-proof casserole on the hob. Cook the lamb, in batches, until browned all over. Remove and set aside.

2 Peel the onions, halve them lengthwise, and cut into thick wedges. Over a medium heat, cook with the garlic in the same dish as you cooked the lamb, stirring continuously until the onion becomes soft and translucent.

3 Return the lamb to the dish and add the carrots, pearl barley, wine, stock, tomatoes, and tomato paste and bring to a boil.

4 Bake, covered with a lid, for 2 hours, stirring occasionally.

5 After 2 hours, remove from the oven, stir in the thyme, and season. Return the dish to the oven and bake uncovered for a further 15 minutes or until the lamb is tender and falling off the bone. Serve with creamy mashed potatoes.

"He was a bold man who first swallowed an oyster."
King James I of Scotland (1394–1437)

MONDAY 27

AM

PM

TUESDAY 28   Mardi Gras

AM

PM

WEDNESDAY 1   Ash Wednesday

AM

PM

THURSDAY 2

AM

PM

FRIDAY 3

AM

PM

QUICK TIP

If you've added too much salt to your casserole, this can be remedied by adding a couple of peeled or quartered potatoes. After a few minutes cooking, remove the potatoes, which should have absorbed some of the excess salt.

	Su	M	T	W	Th	F	S	Su	M	T	W	Th	F	S	Su	M	T	W	Th	F	S	Su	M	T	W	Th	F	S	Su	M	T	W	Th	F	S	Su
FEBRUARY		1	2	3	4	5	6	7	8	9	10	11	12	13	14	15	16	17	18	19	20	21	22	23	24	25	26	27	28							
MARCH		1	2	3	4	5	6	7	8	9	10	11	12	13	14	15	16	17	18	19	20	21	22	23	24	25	26	27	28	29	30	31				
APRIL			1	2	3	4	5	6	7	8	9	10	11	12	13	14	15	16	17	18	19	20	21	22	23	24	25	26	27	28	29	30				

COOK'S PANTRY

BOUQUET GARNI

A bouquet garni is a classic herb mixture that is used to flavor soups, stews, and broths. Tying or bagging the herbs together allows them to be easily removed before the dish is served. Use a length of string to tie together 2–3 sprigs of fresh thyme, 5–6 parsley stalks, and 1 bay leaf. Add to the saucepan or casserole, tying the string to the handle for easy removal. Alternatively, place some dried herbs in a small cheesecloth bag and tie the top with string.

SATURDAY 4

SUNDAY 5

PANTRY RUNNING LOW ON

"Of soup and love, the first is best."

Spanish proverb

MONDAY 6

TUESDAY 7

WEDNESDAY 8

THURSDAY 9

FRIDAY 10

QUICK TIP

Never store your fresh tomatoes in the refrigerator—they will quickly lose their taste and may become spongy. Instead, keep them in a bowl, as you would other fruit, and remember always to wash them before using.

	Su	M	T	W	Th	F	S	Su	M	T	W	Th	F	S	Su	M	T	W	Th	F	S	Su	M	T	W	Th	F	S	Su	M	T	W	Th	F	S	Su
FEBRUARY		1	2	3	4	5	6	7	8	9	10	11	12	13	14	15	16	17	18	19	20	21	22	23	24	25	26	27	28
MARCH		1	2	3	4	5	6	7	8	9	10	11	12	13	14	15	16	17	18	19	20	21	22	23	24	25	26	27	28	29	30	31
APRIL		1	2	3	4	5	6	7	8	9	10	11	12	13	14	15	16	17	18	19	20	21	22	23	24	25	26	27	28	29	30

FOOD IN A FLASH

SPAGHETTI WITH TOMATO, ZUCCHINI, AND RICOTTA

(serves 2)

In a large pot of boiling salted water, cook sufficient spaghetti for 2 people. Meanwhile, heat 2 tablespoons olive oil in a skillet, add 2 zucchini, cut into ½-inch strips, and fry until tender. Add 1 clove garlic, thinly sliced, and a handful of cherry tomatoes. Cook, stirring, until the tomatoes soften and split. Combine this mixture with the drained cooked spaghetti and a handful of arugula in a bowl, and toss. Stir in ½ cup Italian ricotta cheese, season to taste with salt and black pepper, and serve immediately.

SATURDAY 11

SUNDAY 12

PANTRY RUNNING LOW ON

MONDAY 13 Purim begins at sundown

TUESDAY 14

WEDNESDAY 15

THURSDAY 16

FRIDAY 17 St. Patrick's Day

QUICK TIP

To quickly make a pretty, decorative pattern on top of a sponge cake, cheesecake, pie, or tart, simply place a paper doily on top, dust with confectioner's sugar, and carefully lift off the doily.

		Su	M	T	W	Th	F	S	Su	M	T	W	Th	F	S	Su	M	T	W	Th	F	S	Su	M	T	W	Th	F	S	Su	M	T	W	Th	F	S	Su
FEBRUARY			1	2	3	4	5	6	7	8	9	10	11	12	13	14	15	16	17	18	19	20	21	22	23	24	25	26	27	28
MARCH		1	2	3	4	5	6	7	8	9	10	11	12	13	14	15	16	17	18	19	20	21	22	23	24	25	26	27	28	29	30	31
APRIL		1	2	3	4	5	6	7	8	9	10	11	12	13	14	15	16	17	18	19	20	21	22	23	24	25	26	27	28	29	30

COOK'S PANTRY

ROSE PETAL JELLY

This is a fragrant and delicious filling for chocolate cake. Take 1 cup chemical-free, fresh rose petals. Blend them until smooth in a food processor with ¾ cup water and the juice of 1 lemon. Slowly add 2½ cups sugar. Blend until the sugar has dissolved. In a saucepan stir 1 package pectin (such as Sure Jell) into ¾ cup water, bring to a boil, and boil hard for 1 minute. Quickly pour this into the processor and blend again. Pour into a clean jar and let set until firm. This will take at least 6 hours. The jelly will keep for 1 month in the refrigerator.

SATURDAY 18

SUNDAY 19

PANTRY RUNNING LOW ON

MONDAY 20 | First Day of Spring

TUESDAY 21

WEDNESDAY 22

THURSDAY 23

FRIDAY 24

QUICK TIP

When measuring out sticky ingredients such as syrup or honey, first grease the measuring jug or spoon you are using with a little oil or butter. This will ensure that the ingredient pours out more easily.

	Su	M	T	W	Th	F	S	Su	M	T	W	Th	F	S	Su	M	T	W	Th	F	S	Su	M	T	W	Th	F	S	Su	M	T	W	Th	F	S	Su
FEBRUARY		1	2	3	4	5	6	7	8	9	10	11	12	13	14	15	16	17	18	19	20	21	22	23	24	25	26	27	28
MARCH		1	2	3	4	5	6	7	8	9	10	11	12	13	14	15	16	17	18	19	20	21	22	23	24	25	26	27	28	29	30	31
APRIL		1	2	3	4	5	6	7	8	9	10	11	12	13	14	15	16	17	18	19	20	21	22	23	24	25	26	27	28	29	30

FOOD IN A FLASH

WARMED PEACHES WITH MARSALA, MASCARPONE, AND AMARETTI COOKIES

(serves 2)

Cut 4 fresh, ripe peaches in half and remove the pits. Put the peaches in a shallow baking dish, flat side up. Dot ½ tablespoon mascarpone (Italian cream cheese) in the hollow of each peach half. Place under a preheated hot broiler until the mascarpone has melted—about 5 minutes. Remove from the broiler and spoon 2–3 teaspoons sweet (dolce) Marsala wine over each half before sprinkling with crumbled Amaretti di Saronno cookies. Serve immediately.

SATURDAY 25

SUNDAY 26

PANTRY RUNNING LOW ON

Asparagus and Lemon Risotto

WITH GOAT CHEESE AND FRESH HERBS

Risotto and seasonal vegetables are made for each other—never more than when the vegetable is the first asparagus of spring. But preparing this Italian classic intimidates many. Is it "toasting" the rice that's daunting, or achieving the right balance of creaminess and bite? Or is it finding risotto rice in the first place? (If there's none in your local store, you can order it online.) Perhaps it's all the stirring required: it should be slow, sensuous, and deliberate, it is said. Like all the finest things in life, risotto won't be rushed.

INGREDIENTS *Makes 4–6 servings*

3 tbsp olive oil
2 shallots, chopped
1 clove garlic, crushed
1½ cups arborio, or
   risotto, rice

1½ pts vegetable stock
1 bunch asparagus
grated zest and juice of
   half an unwaxed lemon
6 fresh sage leaves, chopped

1 sprig rosemary, finely
   chopped
¼ cup soft goat cheese
salt and black pepper
flat-leaf parsley to garnish

METHOD

1 In a large saucepan, heat the oil and cook the shallots and garlic over medium heat for 4 minutes. Warm the stock in a separate pan.

2 Add the rice to the garlic and shallots, and stir well. Add a little of the stock and stir until the rice has absorbed most of the liquid. Keep adding the stock gradually, for about 10 more minutes, until most of it is gone. Stir constantly.

3 Trim the asparagus and chop it into 2-inch pieces. Add it, along with the lemon zest and herbs, and continue to cook gently, stirring for a further 10 minutes. At no point should you allow the risotto to become too dry—add more stock or water as necessary.

4 When the rice is cooked and has absorbed all the stock, remove from the heat and stir in the goat cheese and lemon juice.

5 Season to taste and garnish with sprigs of flat-leaf parsley before serving.

"Appetite comes with eating."
François Rabelais (1495–1553)

MONDAY 27

TUESDAY 28

WEDNESDAY 29

THURSDAY 30

FRIDAY 31

QUICK TIP

Mince a whole batch of garlic cloves at a time: form the mixture into a log, wrap it tight in plastic wrap, and freeze. Whenever a recipe calls for minced garlic, just cut a slice off the frozen log.

	Su	M	T	W	Th	F	S	Su	M	T	W	Th	F	S	Su	M	T	W	Th	F	S	Su	M	T	W	Th	F	S	Su	M	T	W	Th	F	S	Su
MARCH		1	2	3	4	5	6	7	8	9	10	11	12	13	14	15	16	17	18	19	20	21	22	23	24	25	26	27	28	29	30	31
APRIL						1	2	3	4	5	6	7	8	9	10	11	12	13	14	15	16	17	18	19	20	21	22	23	24	25	26	27	28	29	30
MAY	1	2	3	4	5	6	7	8	9	10	11	12	13	14	15	16	17	18	19	20	21	22	23	24	25	26	27	28	29	30	31

COOK'S PANTRY

PURE CHILI POWDER

Storebought chili powders often contain other flavorings, such as garlic and cumin, so it's better to make your own and add herbs and spices to taste. Place 8 dried chilies in a bowl and pour over hot water. Let soak for 30 minutes, then pat dry. Heat a heavy skillet and dry-fry the chilies until crisp—this will give them a distinctive smoky taste. Let cool slightly, then transfer to a mortar and grind to a fine powder with a pestle. Store in an airtight container.

SATURDAY 1   April Fools' Day

SUNDAY 2   Daylight Saving Time begins

PANTRY RUNNING LOW ON

APRIL 3 – 9

MONDAY 3

AM

PM

TUESDAY 4

AM

PM

WEDNESDAY 5

AM

PM

THURSDAY 6

AM

PM

FRIDAY 7

AM

PM

QUICK TIP

It's always disappointing when an egg breaks in the pan. Stick a pin into the large end of a raw egg to make a very small hole from which air can escape. This will prevent the egg from cracking during boiling.

	Su	M	T	W	Th	F	S	Su	M	T	W	Th	F	S	Su	M	T	W	Th	F	S	Su	M	T	W	Th	F	S	Su	M	T	W	Th	F	S	Su
MARCH		1	2	3	4	5	6	7	8	9	10	11	12	13	14	15	16	17	18	19	20	21	22	23	24	25	26	27	28	29	30	31				
APRIL				1	2	3	4	5	6	7	8	9	10	11	12	13	14	15	16	17	18	19	20	21	22	23	24	25	26	27	28	29	30			
MAY		1	2	3	4	5	6	7	8	9	10	11	12	13	14	15	16	17	18	19	20	21	22	23	24	25	26	27	28	29	30	31				

FOOD IN A FLASH

WARM FAVA BEANS WITH BACON AND FETA
(serves 2)
Cook 2 cups of shelled fresh fava beans in salted water
until tender—about 10 minutes. (If unavailable, use cooked,
canned beans.) Drain and put in a medium bowl. Broil
2 thin slices of bacon until crisp, and chop roughly. Add to
the beans along with ½ cup crumbled Greek feta cheese. Add
1 teaspoon of olive oil or bottled salad dressing to moisten,
and season to taste with salt and black pepper. Serve
immediately with fresh crusty bread.

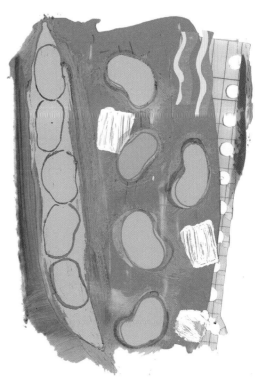

SATURDAY 8

SUNDAY 9   Palm Sunday

PANTRY RUNNING LOW ON

"Cookery has become a noble art, a noble science; cooks are gentlemen."

Robert Burton (1577–1640)

MONDAY 10

TUESDAY 11

WEDNESDAY 12 Passover (Pesach) begins at sundown

THURSDAY 13

FRIDAY 14 Good Friday

QUICK TIP

When making emulsified sauces such as mayonnaise, make sure that all the ingredients are at room temperature before you start.
If eggs are used straight from the refrigerator, your mayonnaise is more likely to curdle.

	Su	M	T	W	Th	F	S	Su	M	T	W	Th	F	S	Su	M	T	W	Th	F	S	Su	M	T	W	Th	F	S	Su	M	T	W	Th	F	S	Su
MARCH		1	2	3	4	5	6	7		8	9	10	11	12	13	14	15	16	17	18	19	20	21	22	23	24	25	26	27	28	29	30	31
APRIL			1	2	3	4		5	6	7	8	9	10	11	12	13	14	15	16	17	18	19	20	21	22	23	24	25	26	27	28	29	30
MAY	1	2	3	4	5	6	7	8	9	10	11	12	13	14	15	16	17	18	19	20	21	22	23	24	25	26	27	28	29	30	31

COOK'S PANTRY

TARRAGON VINEGAR

It's simple to make herbed vinegars at home and they are an excellent way of adding extra flavor to salad dressings, sauces, and soups. Put 3–4 sprigs of fresh tarragon into a clean jar and cover with white wine vinegar. Keep in a warm place for 2–3 weeks, shaking the jar occasionally. Strain the vinegar, then pour into a bottle and add another sprig of fresh tarragon. You can use other herbs such as basil or rosemary in the same way.

SATURDAY 15

SUNDAY 16 Easter Sunday

PANTRY RUNNING LOW ON

"Butter is the oil of the heart."

MONDAY 17

TUESDAY 18

WEDNESDAY 19

THURSDAY 20

FRIDAY 21

QUICK TIP

Once you've separated eggs never leave the yolks exposed to the air—they will quickly develop a tough skin, which can cause problems in some recipes. It's best to put them on a plate and cover the yolks with plastic wrap placed right on their surface.

		Su	M	T	W	Th	F	S	Su	M	T	W	Th	F	S	Su	M	T	W	Th	F	S	Su	M	T	W	Th	F	S	Su	M	T	W	Th	F	S	Su
MARCH			1	2	3	4	5	6	7	8	9	10	11	12	13	14	15	16	17	18	19	20	21	22	23	24	25	26	27	28	29	30	31
APRIL				1	2	3	4	5	6	7	8	9	10	11	12	13	14	15	16	17	18	19	20	21	22	23	24	25	26	27	28	29	30
MAY	1	2	3	4	5	6	7	8	9	10	11	12	13	14	15	16	17	18	19	20	21	22	23	24	25	26	27	28	29	30	31

FOOD IN A FLASH

PARMESAN-CRUMBED LAMB STEAKS
(serves 2)

Take 2 lamb steaks and pound them a little thinner with a rolling pin. Dip each one in a little beaten egg and some all-purpose flour. Next dip them in a mixture of ½ cup fresh white breadcrumbs and ½ cup finely-grated Parmesan cheese. Melt 1 tablespoon of butter in a skillet and fry the crumbed steaks on both sides until golden and cooked through. Serve with fresh lemon wedges on the side and a selection of baby spring vegetables, such as carrots, new potatoes, and peas.

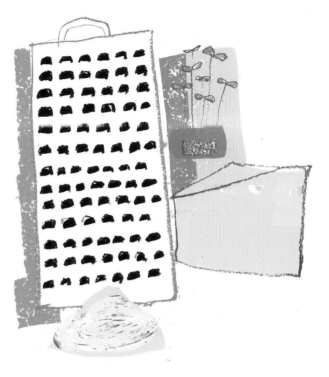

SATURDAY 22	Earth Day		
	AM		PM

SUNDAY 23	Greek Orthodox Easter		
	AM		PM

PANTRY RUNNING LOW ON

"'Tis an ill cook that cannot lick his own fingers."

William Shakespeare (1564–1616)

MONDAY 24

TUESDAY 25

WEDNESDAY 26

THURSDAY 27

FRIDAY 28   National Arbor Day

QUICK TIP

Put a piece of wax paper directly on top of a grater's surface before grating citrus fruits. As you grate, the paper will break up around the grater's teeth but will not shred. The grated zest collects on the wax paper, is easy to transfer to a bowl, and the grater stays clean.

	Su	M	T	W	Th	F	S	Su	M	T	W	Th	F	S	Su	M	T	W	Th	F	S	Su	M	T	W	Th	F	S	Su	M	T	W	Th	F	S	Su
MARCH		1	2	3	4	5	6	7	8	9	10	11	12	13	14	15	16	17	18	19	20	21	22	23	24	25	26	27	28	29	30	31
APRIL			1	2	3	4	5	6	7	8	9	10	11	12	13	14	15	16	17	18	19	20	21	22	23	**24**	**25**	**26**	**27**	**28**	**29**	**30**
MAY	1	2	3	4	5	6	7	8	9	10	11	12	13	14	15	16	17	18	19	20	21	22	23	24	25	26	27	28	29	30	31

COOK'S PANTRY

LEMON CURD

A delicious treat spread on bread or used as a
cake filling. Whisk together ¾ cup fresh lemon juice,
1 tablespoon finely-grated lemon zest, ¾ cup sugar,
and 3 large eggs in a saucepan. Cut 1 stick (½ cup)
unsalted butter into pieces and add to the mixture.
Cook, stirring constantly, over a low heat until the
liquid becomes thick and the first bubble appears on
the surface. Pour into a clean bowl, cover with plastic
wrap, and chill. The lemon curd will keep for up to
1 week in the refrigerator.

SATURDAY 29

AM

PM

SUNDAY 30

AM

PM

PANTRY RUNNING LOW ON

Mini Choux Puffs

WITH STRAWBERRIES AND FRANGIPANI CREAM

How lovely to celebrate Mother's Day by serving afternoon tea. No teatime would be complete without a delicious treat, such as these mini pastry puffs, or *choux*. This recipe calls for frangipani cream with strawberries. Almond-flavored frangipani is named after the Marquese Frangipani, a 16th-century Italian noble who developed a bitter almond fragrance to scent his gloves. Soon it was all the rage in Paris. Inevitably, an edible almond cream followed.

INGREDIENTS *Makes 4 servings (12 puffs)*

½ stick (¼ cup) unsalted butter, cut into cubes (plus extra for greasing)
½ cup water
a pinch of salt

½ cup all-purpose flour
2 large eggs, beaten
1½ cups whipping cream
2 cups fresh strawberries, hulled and chopped

½ tsp almond extract
sugar to taste
confectioner's sugar for dusting

METHOD

1 Preheat oven to 425°F. Grease a baking sheet, run it under water and shake to remove excess (the water turns to steam in the oven, helping the puffs rise.)

2 Place the butter, water, and salt in a heavy saucepan and bring to a boil over high heat. Reduce heat to moderate, add all the flour, and cook, stirring vigorously, until the mixture pulls away from the side of the pan.

3 Remove from the heat and add the beaten eggs, a little at a time, stirring vigorously until the mixture is smooth and glossy.

4 Spoon small mounds of mixture onto the sheet. Bake for 10 minutes, then reduce the temperature to 375°F and bake for 20 minutes more, or until golden. Let the puffs cool on a wire rack before slicing each one in half.

5 Whip the cream, add the strawberries and almond extract, and sweeten to taste. Fill each puff with cream and dust with confectioner's sugar.

"Tell me what you eat, and I will tell you what you are."
Anthelme Brillat-Savarin (1755–1826)

MONDAY 1

AM

PM

TUESDAY 2

AM

PM

WEDNESDAY 3

AM

PM

THURSDAY 4

AM

PM

FRIDAY 5

AM

PM

QUICK TIP

If your pre-prepared choux *pastry buns or ring have gone soft and soggy, they will respond very well to a few minutes back in a hot oven where they will soon crisp up again.*

	Su	M	T	W	Th	F	S	Su	M	T	W	Th	F	S	Su	M	T	W	Th	F	S	Su	M	T	W	Th	F	S	Su	M	T	W	Th	F	S	Su
APRIL						1	2	3	4	5	6	7	8	9	10	11	12	13	14	15	16	17	18	19	20	21	22	23	24	25	26	27	28	29	30
MAY	1	2	3	4	5	6	7	8	9	10	11	12	13	14	15	16	17	18	19	20	21	22	23	24	25	26	27	28	29	30	31
JUNE		1	2	3	4	5	6	7	8	9	10	11	12	13	14	15	16	17	18	19	20	21	22	23	24	25	26	27	28	29	30

FOOD IN A FLASH

BROILED CHICKEN BREASTS WITH HERB AND SHALLOT BUTTER

(serves 2)

Mix together (in a food processor or by hand) 1 stick butter, ½ cup fresh breadcrumbs, 2 shallots, finely chopped, 1 clove garlic, crushed, and 2 tablespoons chopped fresh parsley. Put 2 chicken breasts under the broiler to cook and 5 minutes before they are done remove them from the oven, spread the paste over the top, and return to the broiler for another couple of minutes or until the topping browns. Serve immediately with new potatoes and green beans.

SATURDAY 6

SUNDAY 7

PANTRY RUNNING LOW ON

"There is no such thing as a little garlic."

MONDAY 8

TUESDAY 9

WEDNESDAY 10

THURSDAY 11

FRIDAY 12

QUICK TIP

To get the most juice out of citrus fruits, before juicing roll them on the counter, bearing down hard. An even better method is to microwave a lemon or lime, at medium-high, for 1 minute. Either method increases the juice yield enormously.

	Su	M	T	W	Th	F	S	Su	M	T	W	Th	F	S	Su	M	T	W	Th	F	S	Su	M	T	W	Th	F	S	Su	M	T	W	Th	F	S	Su
APRIL						1	2	3	4	5	6	7	8	9	10	11	12	13	14	15	16	17	18	19	20	21	22	23	24	25	26	27	28	29	30
MAY	1	2	3	4	5	6	7	8	9	10	11	12	13	14	15	16	17	18	19	20	21	22	23	24	25	26	27	28	29	30	31
JUNE			1	2	3	4	5	6	7	8	9	10	11	12	13	14	15	16	17	18	19	20	21	22	23	24	25	26	27	28	29	30

COOK'S PANTRY

STRAWBERRY SYRUP

Perfect poured over ice cream or pancakes. Purée
3 lbs strawberries in a food processor. Pour the
purée through a sieve lined with a double layer of
cheesecloth. Gather up the corners and press gently
to extract as much juice as possible. Measure the
juice and for each 2½ cups put 1 cup sugar into a
saucepan. Add the juice to the pan and heat gently,
stirring until the sugar dissolves. Add the juice of
2 lemons and let cool. Pour into sterilized bottles,
store in the refrigerator, and use within 2 weeks.

SATURDAY 13

SUNDAY 14   Mother's Day

PANTRY RUNNING LOW ON

"Cookies are made with butter and love."
Norwegian proverb

MONDAY 15

AM

PM

TUESDAY 16

AM

PM

WEDNESDAY 17

AM

PM

THURSDAY 18

AM

PM

FRIDAY 19

AM

PM

QUICK TIP

Unless asparagus comes fresh from your garden, the ends will probably be tough. The best way to deal with them is to snap the bottom off the asparagus with your hands, rather than cut them, as they should break at just the point at which they harden.

	Su	M	T	W	Th	F	S	Su	M	T	W	Th	F	S	Su	M	T	W	Th	F	S	Su	M	T	W	Th	F	S	Su	M	T	W	Th	F	S	Su
APRIL						1	2	3	4	5	6	7	8	9	10	11	12	13	14	15	16	17	18	19	20	21	22	23	24	25	26	27	28	29	30	
MAY	1	2	3	4	5	6	7	8	9	10	11	12	13	14	15	16	17	18	19	20	21	22	23	24	25	26	27	28	29	30	31					
JUNE			1	2	3	4	5	6	7	8	9	10	11	12	13	14	15	16	17	18	19	20	21	22	23	24	25	26	27	28	29	30				

FOOD IN A FLASH

BAKED ASPARAGUS WITH PANCETTA

(serves 2)

Preheat oven to 400°F. Boil a bundle of fresh asparagus until just tender. Drain carefully and lay the spears in a shallow baking dish. Melt 1–2 tablespoons butter in a skillet, add ½ cup diced pancetta (salt-cured Italian bacon), and fry until golden. Tip the pancetta and butter over the cooked asparagus, and then sprinkle lightly with ½ cup grated Parmesan cheese. Bake in the oven for 10 minutes until the cheese has melted.

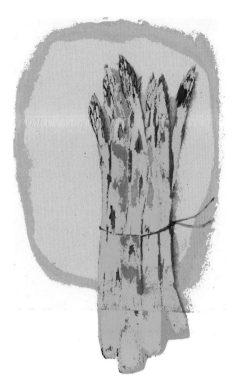

SATURDAY 20   Armed Forces Day (US)

SUNDAY 21

PANTRY RUNNING LOW ON

"There is no such thing as a pretty good omelette."
French proverb

MONDAY 22   Victoria Day (Canada)

TUESDAY 23

WEDNESDAY 24

THURSDAY 25

FRIDAY 26

QUICK TIP

Saffron threads should be steeped in a little warm water or milk until the color of the liquid is even. Add this to a dish toward the end of cooking. Saffron powder can be added to food without soaking, but never to hot oil as it will quickly form into gloopy clumps.

	Su	M	T	W	Th	F	S	Su	M	T	W	Th	F	S	Su	M	T	W	Th	F	S	Su	M	T	W	Th	F	S	Su	M	T	W	Th	F	S	Su
APRIL						1	2	3	4	5	6	7	8	9	10	11	12	13	14	15	16	17	18	19	20	21	22	23	24	25	26	27	28	29	30
MAY	1	2	3	4	5	6	7	8	9	10	11	12	13	14	15	16	17	18	19	20	21	22	23	24	25	26	27	28	29	30	31					
JUNE			1	2	3	4	5	6	7	8	9	10	11	12	13	14	15	16	17	18	19	20	21	22	23	24	25	26	27	28	29	30				

COOK'S PANTRY

LEMONGRASS AND KAFFIR LIME-LEAF OIL

Packed with flavors typical of South-East Asian cuisine, this delicate oil can be used both for cooking and for drizzling over finished dishes. Fill a clean bottle with groundnut oil. Trim and discard the root end from a lemongrass stalk. Lightly bruise the bulbous end and cut the stem into lengths to fit the bottle. Tear 3–4 kaffir lime leaves into pieces and put the lemongrass and lime leaves into the bottle. Cover tightly and leave to infuse in a cool, dark place for 2–3 weeks.

SATURDAY 27

SUNDAY 28

PANTRY RUNNING LOW ON

Seared Salmon

WITH COCONUT SPINACH AND GREEN TEA NOODLES

Is it any wonder that Pan-Asian is the cuisine *du jour*? Drawing on the culinary styles of the entire region, this inventive fare has a taste for every palate, with many healthy ingredients, quick-cooked by methods such as stir-frying and broiling that use little or no oil. The strong flavors of ginger, sesame, chilies, and coconut add punch to many Pan-Asian dishes. For a Father's Day meal, try this spicy seared salmon served on a bed of coconut-flavored spinach with *chasoba*—buckwheat noodles made with green tea.

INGREDIENTS *Makes 4 servings*

4 6-oz salmon fillets	12 oz dried *chasoba* (green tea soba noodles)	2 tbsp Asian chili paste
2 tsp grated ginger	2 garlic cloves, crushed	2 cups coconut cream
1 tbsp sesame oil	2 small red chilies, seeded and finely chopped	3 tbsp lemon juice
2 tbsp soy sauce		2 bunches spinach, stems removed

METHOD

1 Place the salmon fillets in a shallow dish with the ginger, sesame oil, and soy. Allow to marinate for 10 minutes on each side.

2 To cook the noodles, bring a large pot of water to a boil. Add the noodles and stir until it boils again. Reduce to medium-high heat and continue boiling for 5–8 minutes or until the noodles are tender but firm to the bite. Drain in a colander. Rinse thoroughly with warm water. Drain and keep warm.

3 Next make the coconut spinach. Place the garlic, chilies, and chili paste in a saucepan over medium heat and cook for 2 minutes. Add the coconut cream and lemon juice. Simmer for 4 minutes. Add the spinach and toss until wilted.

4 Heat a skillet on high heat and cook each salmon fillet for 1 minute each side.

5 Divide the cooked noodles among 4 serving plates. Place some spinach on each and top with a piece of salmon.

"The art of dining well is no slight art, the pleasure not a slight pleasure."
Michel de Montaigne (1533–1592)

MONDAY 29   Memorial Day

AM

PM

TUESDAY 30

AM

PM

WEDNESDAY 31

AM

PM

THURSDAY 1

AM

PM

FRIDAY 2

AM

PM

QUICK TIP

If you accidentally get your hard-boiled and raw eggs mixed up in the refrigerator, here's how to find out which is which. Place an egg on a flat surface and give it a spin. If it's raw, it will barely turn; if it's cooked, it will spin.

	Su	M	T	W	Th	F	S	Su	M	T	W	Th	F	S	Su	M	T	W	Th	F	S	Su	M	T	W	Th	F	S	Su	M	T	W	Th	F	S	Su	M
MAY		1	2	3	4	5	6	7	8	9	10	11	12	13	14	15	16	17	18	19	20	21	22	23	24	25	26	27	28	29	30	31					
JUNE		1	2	3	4	5	6	7	8	9	10	11	12	13	14	15	16	17	18	19	20	21	22	23	24	25	26	27	28	29	30						
JULY			1	2	3	4	5	6	7	8	9	10	11	12	13	14	15	16	17	18	19	20	21	22	23	24	25	26	27	28	29	30	31				

FOOD IN A FLASH

CHILLED MELON CUPS WITH MUSCAT AND MINT

(serves 2)

Take 1 ripe but firm sweet melon, such as cantaloupe or honeydew. Carefully scoop out approximately 10–15 balls using a melon-baller or spoon. Drop the balls into 2 tall wineglasses (frosted if possible) and then pour over sufficient sweet Muscat grape dessert wine (such as muscatel) to come halfway up the glasses. Add ½ tablespoon chopped fresh mint to each and stir gently using the handle of a fork. Serve very chilled with a small, long-handled spoon.

SATURDAY 3

AM

PM

SUNDAY 4   Pentecost

AM

PM

PANTRY RUNNING LOW ON

MONDAY 5

AM

PM

TUESDAY 6

AM

PM

WEDNESDAY 7

AM

PM

THURSDAY 8

AM

PM

FRIDAY 9

AM

PM

QUICK TIP

When making pesto, first blanch the fresh basil in boiling salted water, then shock it in iced water, drain it, and squeeze it dry. The pesto will stay a brilliant green color for much longer.

	Su	M	T	W	Th	F	S	Su	M	T	W	Th	F	S	Su	M	T	W	Th	F	S	Su	M	T	W	Th	F	S	Su	M	T	W	Th	F	S	Su	M
MAY		1	2	3	4	5	6	7	8	9	10	11	12	13	14	15	16	17	18	19	20	21	22	23	24	25	26	27	28	29	30	31					
JUNE				1	2	3	4	5	6	7	8	9	10	11	12	13	14	15	16	17	18	19	20	21	22	23	24	25	26	27	28	29	30				
JULY					1	2	3	4	5	6	7	8	9	10	11	12	13	14	15	16	17	18	19	20	21	22	23	24	25	26	27	28	29	30	31		

COOK'S PANTRY

FRESH PESTO SAUCE

Nothing you can buy tastes as good as homemade pesto. This quantity is enough to dress pasta for 4–6 servings. Crush 4 cups fresh basil leaves, ¼ cup pine nuts, 2 garlic cloves, peeled, and a pinch of salt in a mortar with a pestle. Transfer to a bowl and work in ⅔ cup finely-grated fresh Parmesan cheese. Slowly add about ½ cup olive oil, stirring well with a wooden spoon. Store for up to 1 month in a sealed jar in the refrigerator, or freeze.

SATURDAY 10

AM

PM

SUNDAY 11

AM

PM

PANTRY RUNNING LOW ON

JUNE 12 – 18

"To eat is a necessity, but to eat intelligently is an art."

La Rochefoucauld (1613–1680)

MONDAY 12

AM

PM

TUESDAY 13

AM

PM

WEDNESDAY 14 Flag Day

AM

PM

THURSDAY 15

AM

PM

FRIDAY 16

AM

PM

QUICK TIP

The easiest way to peel an avocado is to cut it in half lengthwise, slightly twist the two halves, separate them, and remove the pit. Start at the small end and remove the skin with a knife.

	Su	M	T	W	Th	F	S	Su	M	T	W	Th	F	S	Su	M	T	W	Th	F	S	Su	M	T	W	Th	F	S	Su	M	T	W	Th	F	S	Su	M
MAY		1	2	3	4	5	6	7	8	9	10	11	12	13	14	15	16	17	18	19	20	21	22	23	24	25	26	27	28	29	30	31					
JUNE			1	2	3	4	5	6	7	8	9	10	11	12	13	14	15	16	17	18	19	20	21	22	23	24	25	26	27	28	29	30					
JULY				1	2	3	4	5	6	7	8	9	10	11	12	13	14	15	16	17	18	19	20	21	22	23	24	25	26	27	28	29	30	31			

FOOD IN A FLASH

LAMB AND MANGO SALAD WITH SWEET CHILI DRESSING
(serves 2)
Brush a 10-oz boneless lamb steak with ½ tablespoon sesame oil and cook on a heated oiled grill plate or barbecue until browned and cooked as desired. Combine ½ red onion, sliced thinly, 1 medium mango, peeled, pitted, and sliced, 1 cup cherry tomatoes, halved, ½ cup mung bean sprouts, and ½ cup chopped cilantro in a salad bowl. Thinly slice the lamb, add to the bowl, and toss through with ⅛ cup ready-made Asian-style sweet chili sauce and ½ tablespoon white rice vinegar. Serve immediately.

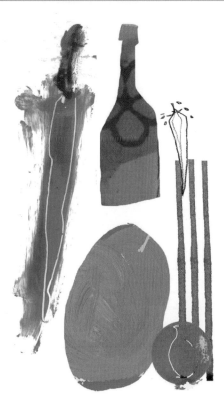

SATURDAY 17

AM

PM

SUNDAY 18   Father's Day

AM

PM

PANTRY RUNNING LOW ON

"A good meal ought to begin with hunger."
French proverb

MONDAY 19

AM

PM

TUESDAY 20

AM

PM

WEDNESDAY 21   First Day of Summer

AM

PM

THURSDAY 22

AM

PM

FRIDAY 23

AM

PM

QUICK TIP

When sautéing or stir-frying any dish always preheat the pan well before adding oil. If you heat the oil at the same time as the pan, the food you cook will be far more likely to stick.

	Su	M	T	W	Th	F	S	Su	M	T	W	Th	F	S	Su	M	T	W	Th	F	S	Su	M	T	W	Th	F	S	Su	M
MAY	1	2	3	4	5	6	7	8	9	10	11	12	13	14	15	16	17	18	19	20	21	22	23	24	25	26	27	28	29	30	31
JUNE		1	2	3	4	5	6	7	8	9	10	11	12	13	14	15	16	17	18	19	20	21	22	23	24	25	26	27	28	29	30
JULY		1	2	3	4	5	6	7	8	9	10	11	12	13	14	15	16	17	18	19	20	21	22	23	24	25	26	27	28	29	30	31

COOK'S PANTRY

ROASTED SESAME SEEDS

The flavor of sesame seeds is much improved by roasting them in a dry skillet. Once roasted and cooled they can be stored in an airtight container and used to sprinkle over stir-fries, Asian noodle dishes, or hummus just before serving. Spread out a spoonful or two of seeds in a thin layer on the base of a large, non-stick skillet. Cook over a low to medium heat for 2–3 minutes, gently tossing the seeds frequently until they are golden brown.

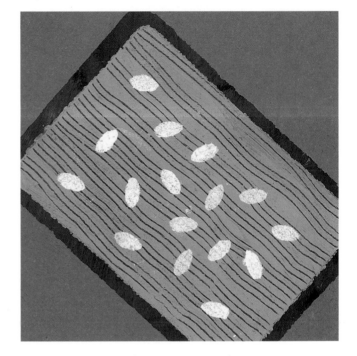

SATURDAY 24

AM

PM

SUNDAY 25

AM

PM

PANTRY RUNNING LOW ON

Grilled Steak Sandwich

WITH AIOLI AND ARUGULA AND FENNEL SALAD

The Fourth of July barbecue doesn't have to mean the same old hotdogs and burgers on squishy buns. For a change, serve tasty grilled steak and tomato sandwiches on ciabatta—rustic Italian bread—spread with aioli, a classic garlic mayonnaise. To be sure the fire is ready, perform the "three-second test": Hold your hand six inches above the charcoal. If you can keep it there for three seconds, the temperature's just right. Once food goes on the grill, keep a close eye on it, as grilling times can only be approximate.

INGREDIENTS *Serves 4*

3 large fennel bulbs
12 oz arugula
½ cup good-quality
   mayonnaise
2 cloves garlic, crushed

4 beef fillet steaks
   (3–4 oz each)
2 large globe tomatoes,
   halved
3 tbsp olive oil

4 thick slices ciabatta
   (rustic Italian) bread
2 tbsp fresh basil, shredded
1 tbsp balsamic vinegar
salt and black pepper

METHOD

1 To make the salad, trim the fennel and remove the outside layer. Slice the bulbs into quarters and then into thin crescents. Combine the fennel with the arugula in a large salad bowl. Cover and set aside.

2 To make the aioli, combine the mayonnaise and garlic in a bowl. Set aside.

3 Cook the beef on a heated and oiled grill pan, or grill on the barbecue, for 2 minutes on each side for a medium-cooked steak. Let it rest for 5 minutes.

4 Meanwhile, place the tomatoes, cut side up, on a broiler pan and drizzle a tablespoon of the olive oil over them. Broil for 10 minutes until softened.

5 To assemble the sandwiches, toast the ciabatta, spread each slice with aioli, top with a steak and a tomato half, and sprinkle with basil.

6 Whisk the remaining oil and balsamic vinegar in a bowl, season to taste, pour over the salad, and toss well. Serve on the side with the steak sandwiches.

"Let food be thy medicine, thy medicine shall be thy food."
Hippocrates (c.460–377BCE)

MONDAY 26

AM

PM

TUESDAY 27

AM

PM

WEDNESDAY 28

AM

PM

THURSDAY 29

AM

PM

FRIDAY 30

AM

PM

QUICK TIP

Salad greens are fragile and can easily be damaged. When washing them never hold them directly under a running faucet. Always dip and wash them carefully in a large bowl of water and lift out onto paper towels to dry.

	Su	M	T	W	Th	F	S	Su	M	T	W	Th	F	S	Su	M	T	W	Th	F	S	Su	M	T	W	Th	F	S	Su	M	T	W	Th	F	S	Su	M
JUNE			1	2	3	4	5	6	7	8	9	10	11	12	13	14	15	16	17	18	19	20	21	22	23	24	25	26	27	28	29	30
JULY			1	2	3	4	5	6	7	8	9	10	11	12	13	14	15	16	17	18	19	20	21	22	23	24	25	26	27	28	29	30	31
AUGUST	1	2	3	4	5	6	7	8	9	10	11	12	13	14	15	16	17	18	19	20	21	22	23	24	25	26	27	28	29	30	31

FOOD IN A FLASH

TOMATO AND PESTO TARTLETS

(serves 2)

Preheat oven to 450°F and heat a large baking sheet. Cut 5 oz defrosted ready-made puff pastry into 2 pieces of equal size. Roll each piece out on a floured counter until it is large enough for you to cut it into a 7-inch flat round. (You can turn up the edges slightly if you prefer.) Use a small plate as a guide. Prick with a fork, spread 1 tablespoon of pesto (see recipe for June 5–11) over each, top with overlapping slices of fresh tomato, brush with olive oil, and season to taste with salt and black pepper. Slide onto the preheated baking sheet and cook for 15 minutes or until golden brown. Sprinkle with chopped fresh basil, and serve immediately.

SATURDAY 1	Canada Day

AM / PM

SUNDAY 2	

AM / PM

PANTRY RUNNING LOW ON

JULY 3 – 9

"Fish, to taste right, must swim three times—in water, in butter, and in wine."

Polish proverb

MONDAY 3

AM

PM

TUESDAY 4   Independence Day

AM

PM

WEDNESDAY 5

AM

PM

THURSDAY 6

AM

PM

FRIDAY 7

AM

PM

QUICK TIP

If you can't find canned coconut milk in your local store, it's easy to make your own. Place some shredded coconut in a jug and pour over boiling water. Allow to stand for 20 minutes, strain, and use.

	Su	M	T	W	Th	F	S	Su	M	T	W	Th	F	S	Su	M	T	W	Th	F	S	Su	M	T	W	Th	F	S	Su	M	T	W	Th	F	S	Su	M

JUNE   1 2 3 4 5 6 7 8 9 10 11 12 13 14 15 16 17 18 19 20 21 22 23 24 25 26 27 28 29 30
JULY   1 2 3 4 5 6 7 8 9 10 11 12 13 14 15 16 17 18 19 20 21 22 23 24 25 26 27 28 29 30 31
AUGUST 1 2 3 4 5 6 7 8 9 10 11 12 13 14 15 16 17 18 19 20 21 22 23 24 25 26 27 28 29 30 31

COOK'S PANTRY

HERB AND SAFFRON OIL

A light and delicious oil that's great for making salad dressings and mayonnaise, for dressing cooked vegetables, and for brushing on foods before broiling, roasting, or barbecuing. Wrap ½ teaspoon of saffron strands in a small piece of kitchen foil and heat gently in a heavy skillet for about 3 minutes. Unwrap the saffron, put into a clean bottle, and add 2 sprigs of fresh rosemary, 2 sprigs of fresh tarragon, 2 bay leaves, 4⅓ cups olive oil, and ⅔ cup walnut oil. Let infuse for 2–3 weeks in a cool, dark place.

SATURDAY 8

AM

PM

SUNDAY 9

AM

PM

PANTRY RUNNING LOW ON

"A man seldom thinks with more earnestness of anything than he does of his dinner."
Dr. Samuel Johnson (1709–1784)

MONDAY 10

AM

PM

TUESDAY 11

AM

PM

WEDNESDAY 12

AM

PM

THURSDAY 13

AM

PM

FRIDAY 14

AM

PM

QUICK TIP

To speed the ripening process of an avocado, place the fruit in a paper bag and store at room temperature until ready to eat (usually two to five days). Putting an apple or banana in with the avocado speeds up the process even more.

FOOD IN A FLASH

COCONUT BEEF SKEWERS

(serves 2)

Slice 1½ lbs trimmed round or sirloin steak into long, thick strips and thread them onto 4 metal kebab (kabob) skewers. Combine 1 tablespoon curry paste (preferably red Thai) with ⅓ cup canned coconut cream and ¼ cup shredded coconut, and spread over the meat. Place the skewers of meat on a preheated hot broiler or barbecue and cook for 2 minutes on each side or until the meat is cooked as desired. Serve immediately with a green salad.

SATURDAY 15

AM

PM

SUNDAY 16

AM

PM

PANTRY RUNNING LOW ON

"Give me neither poverty nor riches; feed me with food convenient for me."

Proverbs 30:8

MONDAY 17

TUESDAY 18

WEDNESDAY 19

THURSDAY 20

FRIDAY 21

QUICK TIP

When grilling raw sausages on the barbecue, first poach them three-quarters of the way through (takes about 10–15 minutes), and then finish them off on the grill. The outsides will be nicely browned and the insides will be fully cooked.

	Su	M	T	W	Th	F	S	Su	M	T	W	Th	F	S	Su	M	T	W	Th	F	S	Su	M	T	W	Th	F	S	Su	M	T	W	Th	F	S	Su	M
JUNE			1	2	3	4	5	6	7	8	9	10	11	12	13	14	15	16	17	18	19	20	21	22	23	24	25	26	27	28	29	30				
JULY				1	2	3	4	5	6	7	8	9	10	11	12	13	14	15	16	17	18	19	20	21	22	23	24	25	26	27	28	29	30	31		
AUGUST	1	2	3	4	5	6	7	8	9	10	11	12	13	14	15	16	17	18	19	20	21	22	23	24	25	26	27	28	29	30	31					

COOK'S PANTRY

FRESH HERB ICE CUBES

Freezing is an excellent way of preserving delicate fresh herbs that cannot be successfully dried—such as basil, chives, tarragon, chervil, cilantro, dill, and parsley. They will lose their fresh appearance, but will still be suitable for use in cooking. Half-fill ice-cube trays with freshly-chopped herbs and top up with water. Freeze, then remove the cubes from the tray and place in freezer bags. To use, simply add the appropriate number of frozen cubes to soups, stews, and stocks, and heat until melted. They will keep for 3 months in the freezer.

SATURDAY 22

AM

PM

SUNDAY 23

AM

PM

PANTRY RUNNING LOW ON

"Rice is born in water and must die in wine."

MONDAY 24

AM

PM

TUESDAY 25

AM

PM

WEDNESDAY 26

AM

PM

THURSDAY 27

AM

PM

FRIDAY 28

AM

PM

QUICK TIP

Always shuck sweetcorn at the very last moment. To remove the kernels easily and safely hold the cob vertically and run a sharp knife down behind the kernels. Cook and serve immediately.

	Su	M	T	W	Th	F	S	Su	M	T	W	Th	F	S	Su	M	T	W	Th	F	S	Su	M	T	W	Th	F	S	Su	M	T	W	Th	F	S	Su	M
JUNE		1	2	3	4	5	6	7	8	9	10	11	12	13	14	15	16	17	18	19	20	21	22	23	24	25	26	27	28	29	30					
JULY			1	2	3	4	5	6	7	8	9	10	11	12	13	14	15	16	17	18	19	20	21	22	23	24	25	26	27	28	29	30	31			
AUGUST	1	2	3	4	5	6	7	8	9	10	11	12	13	14	15	16	17	18	19	20	21	22	23	24	25	26	27	28	29	30	31					

FOOD IN A FLASH

CHICKEN, ORANGE, AND WATERCRESS SALAD
(serves 2)

Roast or broil 2 chicken breasts. Discard the skin and slice them. Fill a medium salad bowl with peppery salad leaves (such as watercress and arugula) and lay slices of peeled orange and the chicken on top. Make a simple vinaigrette by combining 2 tablespoons extra-virgin olive oil with 2 tablespoons fresh orange juice, 1 teaspoon raspberry vinegar (see recipe for 14–20 August) and 1 tablespoon finely-chopped cilantro. Season dressing to taste with salt and black pepper, and toss through the salad. Serve immediately.

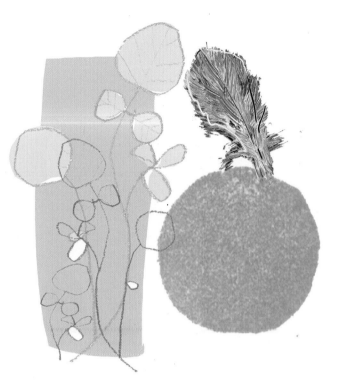

SATURDAY 29

A M   P M

SUNDAY 30

A M   P M

PANTRY RUNNING LOW ON

Summer Salad

HEIRLOOM TOMATOES, BUFFALO MOZZARELLA, AND BLOOD ORANGES WITH HERBED VINAIGRETTE

Nothing says summer like luscious ripe tomatoes. With thousands of heirloom varieties now grown in the U.S., flavorful tomatoes are as close as your garden or farmers' market. Heirloom produce recalls the days before mass farming, when pure strains of vine-ripened tomatoes were the norm. Many varieties date back to the 1800s. The spectacular colors are outdone only by the taste and succulence of the fruit. Favorite "slicers" like Brandywine, Caspian Pink, and Green Zebra need nothing more than a light vinaigrette dressing—if that.

INGREDIENTS *Makes 6 servings*

2 tbsp white wine vinegar	1½ tsp each finely-chopped	2 blood oranges
½ tsp Dijon mustard	flat-leaf parsley, chives,	3 lbs heirloom tomatoes
salt and black pepper	fresh tarragon, and	2 8-oz balls buffalo
½ cup extra-virgin olive oil	fresh chervil	mozzarella

METHOD

1 To make the dressing, combine the vinegar and mustard in a medium bowl and season to taste with salt and pepper. Add the olive oil in a stream, whisking, and continue to whisk the dressing until it is emulsified. Stir in the parsley, chives, tarragon, and chervil. Cover and set aside.

2 Remove the peel and white pith from the oranges. Cut between orange membranes to release the segments into a bowl.

3 Wash the tomatoes and cut in ½-inch wedges, or halves if small.

4 Drain the mozzarella and cut each ball into six slices.

5 Assemble the salad on individual plates by arranging the tomatoes first. Lay two slices of mozzarella on top. Place the orange segments on top of the mozzarella, and spoon over the herbed dressing to finish.

JULY 31 – 6 AUGUST

"When diet is wrong, medicine is of no use. When diet is correct, medicine is of no need."

Ancient Ayurvedic proverb

MONDAY 31

AM

PM

TUESDAY 1

AM

PM

WEDNESDAY 2

AM

PM

THURSDAY 3

AM

PM

FRIDAY 4

AM

PM

QUICK TIP

Be sure to distinguish between marinade and barbecue sauce. A marinade should not include ingredients that will burn. A barbecue sauce can contain sugar, but don't brush it on until a few minutes before you are taking the meat off the broiler.

	Su	M	T	W	Th	F	S	Su	M	T	W	Th	F	S	Su	M	T	W	Th	F	S	Su	M	T	W	Th	F	S	Su	M	T	W	Th	F	S	Su	M
JULY			1	2	3	4	5	6	7	8	9	10	11	12	13	14	15	16	17	18	19	20	21	22	23	24	25	26	27	28	29	30	**31**
AUGUST	1	2	3	4	5	6	7	8	9	10	11	12	13	14	15	16	17	18	19	20	21	22	23	24	25	26	27	28	29	30	31
SEPTEMBER	1	2	3	4	5	6	7	8	9	10	11	12	13	14	15	16	17	18	19	20	21	22	23	24	25	26	27	28	29	30

COOK'S PANTRY

HOMEMADE TOMATO KETCHUP

This tastes so much better than storebought ketchup and helps use up tomatoes if you grow your own and have a glut. Cut 6 lbs tomatoes into quarters and put in a large pan with 1 oz salt and 2½ cups white wine vinegar. Simmer until the tomatoes are soft, then strain through coarse cheesecloth. Return to the pan, add 1 cup sugar, and simmer until the ketchup starts to thicken. Add ½ teaspoon each of ground cloves, allspice, cinnamon, and cayenne. Pour into sterilized bottles and store in the refrigerator. It will last up to 3 weeks.

SATURDAY 5

SUNDAY 6

PANTRY RUNNING LOW ON

"There is no love sincerer than the love of food."
George Bernard Shaw (1856–1950)

MONDAY 7

TUESDAY 8

WEDNESDAY 9

THURSDAY 10

FRIDAY 11

QUICK TIP

*To pit olives rapidly, tap each olive with a mallet or hammer just hard enough to break the skin but not hard enough to crack the pit.
The flesh can then be pulled off easily.*

		Su	M	T	W	Th	F	S	Su	M	T	W	Th	F	S	Su	M	T	W	Th	F	S	Su	M	T	W	Th	F	S	Su	M
JULY							1	2	3	4	5	6	7	8	9	10	11	12	13	14	15	16	17	18	19	20	21	22	23	24	25	26	27	28	29	30	31
AUGUST	1	2	3	4	5	6	7	8	9	10	11	12	13	14	15	16	17	18	19	20	21	22	23	24	25	26	27	28	29	30	31
SEPTEMBER		1	2	3	4	5	6	7	8	9	10	11	12	13	14	15	16	17	18	19	20	21	22	23	24	25	26	27	28	29	30

FOOD IN A FLASH

PASTA SALAD "NIÇOISE-STYLE"
(serves 2)
Cook sufficient penne pasta for 2 people in a large pot
of boiling salted water. Add 1 cup trimmed green beans
to the pan toward the end of the cooking time. When both
pasta and beans are cooked, drain and toss with a small
can of drained tuna fish, 3 tablespoons fresh lemon juice,
2 tablespoons extra-virgin olive oil, ¼ cup chopped fresh
flat-leaf parsley, 1 red onion, finely sliced, 2 tablespoons
pitted black olives, and 1 tablespoon capers. Season to taste
with salt and black pepper, and serve either warm or cold.

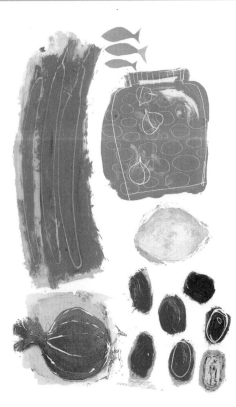

SATURDAY 12

SUNDAY 13

PANTRY RUNNING LOW ON

AUGUST 14 – 20

"Coffee should be black as hell, strong as death, and sweet as love."

Turkish proverb

MONDAY 14

TUESDAY 15

WEDNESDAY 16

THURSDAY 17

FRIDAY 18

QUICK TIP

Yogurt is a useful ingredient but does not always respond well to heating. High-fat yogurts are more stable, but it is possible to stabilize a low-fat yogurt by stirring in a little cornstarch, first blended into a paste with water, before cooking.

	Su	M	T	W	Th	F	S	Su	M	T	W	Th	F	S	Su	M	T	W	Th	F	S	Su	M	T	W	Th	F	S	Su	M	T	W	Th	F	S	Su	M
JULY								1	2	3	4	5	6	7	8	9	10	11	12	13	14	15	16	17	18	19	20	21	22	23	24	25	26	27	28	29	30	31
AUGUST	1	2	3	4	5	6	7	8	9	10	11	12	13	14	15	16	17	18	19	20	21	22	23	24	25	26	27	28	29	30	31						
SEPTEMBER		1	2	3	4	5	6	7	8	9	10	11	12	13	14	15	16	17	18	19	20	21	22	23	24	25	26	27	28	29	30						

COOK'S PANTRY

RASPBERRY VINEGAR

Lovely in salad dressings and also a delicious addition to basting mixtures for roasting ham or duck. Put 1 lb fresh raspberries in a bowl. Measure out 2 cups white wine vinegar and add a little of this to the raspberries. Mash with a wooden spoon. Add the remaining vinegar and stir. Cover the bowl with plastic wrap and leave for 2–3 weeks, stirring occasionally. Strain through 2 layers of cheesecloth and pour into a saucepan. Add ½ cup superfine sugar and heat gently, stirring, until the sugar has dissolved. Simmer for 10 minutes and let cool before pouring into a clean bottle. Store in a cool, dark place and use within 1 year.

SATURDAY 19

SUNDAY 20

PANTRY RUNNING LOW ON

"I doubt whether the world holds for anyone a more soul-stirring surprise than the first adventure with ice-cream."

Heywood Broun (1888–1939)

MONDAY 21

TUESDAY 22

WEDNESDAY 23

THURSDAY 24

FRIDAY 25

QUICK TIP

To remove the odor of raw fish from hands, utensils, and cutting boards, rub with a cut half-lemon. If you are using fresh lemon juice in a dish, once you have squeezed out the juice you can save the lemon halves for this purpose.

	Su	M	T	W	Th	F	S	Su	M	T	W	Th	F	S	Su	M	T	W	Th	F	S	Su	M	T	W	Th	F	S	Su	M	T	W	Th	F	S	Su	M
JULY						1	2	3	4	5	6	7	8	9	10	11	12	13	14	15	16	17	18	19	20	21	22	23	24	25	26	27	28	29	30	31
AUGUST	1	2	3	4	5	6	7	8	9	10	11	12	13	14	15	16	17	18	19	20	21	22	23	24	25	26	27	28	29	30	31						
SEPTEMBER		1	2	3	4	5	6	7	8	9	10	11	12	13	14	15	16	17	18	19	20	21	22	23	24	25	26	27	28	29	30						

FOOD IN A FLASH

COD AND CREAMY SPINACH "GRATIN"
(serves 2)

Blanch 8 oz well-washed fresh spinach in boiling water. Lift out, drain, and chop. Mix with ½ teaspoon nutmeg, 3 tablespoons heavy cream, and ¼ cup finely grated Parmesan cheese, and put to one side. Broil 2 cod fillets (or any firm white fish, such as haddock or hake) under a medium-hot broiler for 3 minutes on each side and place in a shallow baking dish. Top with the spinach, return to the broiler, and cook until golden. Serve immediately with broiled fresh tomatoes.

SATURDAY 26

AM

PM

SUNDAY 27

AM

PM

PANTRY RUNNING LOW ON

Apple Tarte Tatin

WITH CINNAMON CREAM

This classic French apple tart, the tarte tatin, was first served in the late 1800s by sisters Caroline and Stéphanie Tatin at their Loire Valley hotel. One night Stéphanie, running late, had to make a speedy dessert for her guests. She sliced some apples, tossed them into a tart mold with sugar and butter, and popped the pan into the oven. Too late, she realized she'd forgotten the dough. In desperation, she patted dough on top of the pan, then stuck it back to finish baking. To serve, she slapped a plate on top of the mold, tipped it up, and *voilà*—out came the now famous upside-down tart.

INGREDIENTS *Makes 6–8 servings*

1 frozen puff pastry sheet, thawed

½ stick (¼ cup) unsalted butter, softened

½ cup sugar

7–9 Gala apples (3–4 lbs), peeled, quartered lengthwise, and cored

1 cup heavy cream

1 tbsp superfine sugar

1 tsp ground cinnamon

METHOD

1 Preheat oven to 425°F. Roll the pastry into a 10½-inch square. Cut a 10-inch round with a knife, using a plate as a guide. Transfer to a plate and chill.

2 Spread the butter on the bottom and sides of a 10-inch cast-iron skillet and pour the sugar evenly over the base. Arrange the apple in circles. Cook over moderately high heat, undisturbed, until the juices are bubbling.

3 Put the skillet in the oven. Bake for 20 minutes, then remove and lay the pastry over the apples. Return to oven and bake for a further 20–25 minutes until pastry is browned. Transfer skillet to a rack and cool for 10 minutes.

4 Meanwhile, pour the cream into a bowl. Mix together the sugar and cinnamon, add to the cream, and whip until the mixture is thick but not dry.

5 Place a serving plate over the skillet and invert the tart onto the plate. Serve immediately with cinnamon cream on the side.

"Eat at pleasure, drink by measure."

MONDAY 28

AM

PM

TUESDAY 29

AM

PM

WEDNESDAY 30

AM

PM

THURSDAY 31

AM

PM

FRIDAY 1

AM

PM

QUICK TIP

If an emulsified sauce such as Hollandaise or Beurre Blanc appears to be turning greasy or showing signs of curdling, simply drop an ice cube into the sauce and whisk thoroughly until it is smooth—the sauce should re-combine.

	Su	M	T	W	Th	F	S	Su	M	T	W	Th	F	S	Su	M	T	W	Th	F	S	Su	M	T	W	Th	F	S	Su	M	T	W	Th	F	S
AUGUST		1	2	3	4	5	6	7	8	9	10	11	12	13	14	15	16	17	18	19	20	21	22	23	24	25	26	27	28	29	30	31			
SEPTEMBER			1	2	3	4	5	6	7	8	9	10	11	12	13	14	15	16	17	18	19	20	21	22	23	24	25	26	27	28	29	30			
OCTOBER	1	2	3	4	5	6	7	8	9	10	11	12	13	14	15	16	17	18	19	20	21	22	23	24	25	26	27	28	29	30	31				

COOK'S PANTRY

HERBED BUTTERS

Herbed butters are delicious with broiled fish or meat. Put 4 oz (½ cup) sweet butter in a bowl and beat with a wooden spoon or an electric beater until soft. Add 2–4 tablespoons chopped fresh herbs of your choice (such as basil, cilantro, or sage) and season with salt, black pepper, and a dash of freshly-squeezed lemon juice. Beat to mix. Transfer the butter to a piece of waxed paper and shape into a roll. Wrap and chill. Serve cut into slices.

SATURDAY 2

SUNDAY 3

PANTRY RUNNING LOW ON

"It is a difficult matter to argue with the belly since it has no ears."
Cato the Elder (234-149BCE)

MONDAY 4   Labor Day

TUESDAY 5

WEDNESDAY 6

THURSDAY 7

FRIDAY 8

QUICK TIP

The simplest and quickest way to strip any type of currant (red, white, or black) is with a fork. Hold the bunch of currants firmly by the stem and strip off the berries downwards with the fork's tines.

	Su	M	T	W	Th	F	S	Su	M	T	W	Th	F	S	Su	M	T	W	Th	F	S	Su	M	T	W	Th	F	S	Su	M	T	W	Th	F	S
AUGUST		1	2	3	4	5	6	7	8	9	10	11	12	13	14	15	16	17	18	19	20	21	22	23	24	25	26	27	28	29	30	31			
SEPTEMBER				1	2	3	4	5	6	7	8	9	10	11	12	13	14	15	16	17	18	19	20	21	22	23	24	25	26	27	28	29	30		
OCTOBER	1	2	3	4	5	6	7	8	9	10	11	12	13	14	15	16	17	18	19	20	21	22	23	24	25	26	27	28	29	30	31				

FOOD IN A FLASH

GARBANZO BEAN AND GOAT CHEESE FELAFEL

(serves 2)

Place 2 cans (14 oz each) drained garbanzo beans, ½ red onion, finely chopped, 1½ cups fresh breadcrumbs, ½ cup each finely-chopped fresh cilantro, mint, and flat-leaf parsley, and 2 teaspoons ground cumin in a food processor and process until finely chopped. Shape into rounded patties with a small piece of goat cheese inside each patty, then refrigerate for 30 minutes. Fry in a little hot peanut oil until golden and drain on a paper towel. Serve immediately in a warmed pitta bread pocket with mixed salad.

SATURDAY 9

SUNDAY 10

PANTRY RUNNING LOW ON

"Unless the kettle boiling be, filling the teapot spoils the tea."

MONDAY 11

TUESDAY 12

WEDNESDAY 13

THURSDAY 14

FRIDAY 15

QUICK TIP

To give a chilled soufflé the appearance of its baked counterpart, tape a strip of baking parchment around the inside of the soufflé dish before filling it with mixture. Refrigerate and once it has set turn it out onto a plate and peel the paper off carefully.

	Su	M	T	W	Th	F	S	Su	M	T	W	Th	F	S	Su	M	T	W	Th	F	S	Su	M	T	W	Th	F	S	Su	M	T	W	Th	F	S
AUGUST		1	2	3	4	5	6	7	8	9	10	11	12	13	14	15	16	17	18	19	20	21	22	23	24	25	26	27	28	29	30	31		
SEPTEMBER			1	2	3	4	5	6	7	8	9	10	11	12	13	14	15	16	17	18	19	20	21	22	23	24	25	26	27	28	29	30		
OCTOBER		1	2	3	4	5	6	7	8	9	10	11	12	13	14	15	16	17	18	19	20	21	22	23	24	25	26	27	28	29	30	31		

COOK'S PANTRY

RASPBERRY COULIS

This simple sauce is classically spooned over a lightly-poached peach in peach melba, but it is good served with any number of other desserts such as chocolate cake or ice cream. Put a suitable quantity of fresh raspberries in a bowl and crush to a purée with a fork. Tip the purée into a sieve set over a large bowl. Rub through to remove the pips, using the back of a large spoon. Sweeten to taste with confectioner's sugar and stir. Store in the refrigerator and use within 1-2 days, or freeze until required.

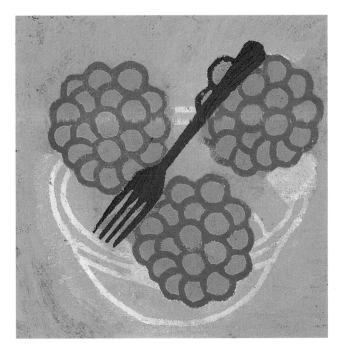

SATURDAY 16

SUNDAY 17

PANTRY RUNNING LOW ON

"Music with dinner is an insult both to the cook and the violinist."

G. K. Chesterton (1874–1936)

MONDAY 18

TUESDAY 19

WEDNESDAY 20

THURSDAY 21

FRIDAY 22

Rosh Hashanah (Jewish New Year)
begins at sundown

QUICK TIP

Wrapping your fresh head of broccoli in a wet cloth before storing it in your refrigerator will keep the vegetable green and moist for much longer and will prevent it from yellowing.

	Su	M	T	W	Th	F	S	Su	M	T	W	Th	F	S	Su	M	T	W	Th	F	S	Su	M	T	W	Th	F	S	Su	M	T	W	Th	F	S
AUGUST		1	2	3	4	5	6	7	8	9	10	11	12	13	14	15	16	17	18	19	20	21	22	23	24	25	26	27	28	29	30	31			
SEPTEMBER			1	2	3	4	5	6	7	8	9	10	11	12	13	14	15	16	17	18	19	20	21	22	23	24	25	26	27	28	29	30			
OCTOBER	1	2	3	4	5	6	7	8	9	10	11	12	13	14	15	16	17	18	19	20	21	22	23	24	25	26	27	28	29	30	31				

FOOD IN A FLASH

LINGUINE WITH SPICY SHRIMP

(serves 2)

Cook sufficient linguine pasta for 2 people in a large pot of boiling salted water. Meanwhile, heat ⅓ cup olive oil in a large skillet. Add 2 cups small peeled shrimp, 3 small, fresh red chilies, finely chopped, and 1 clove garlic, crushed. Cook, stirring continuously, until the shrimp are cooked through. Remove from the heat and stir in ¼ cup chopped fresh flat-leaf parsley and 2 teaspoons grated lemon rind (from an unwaxed lemon). Combine with the cooked pasta and toss gently before serving immediately.

SATURDAY 23 First Day of Autumn

SUNDAY 24

PANTRY RUNNING LOW ON

Pumpkin Casserole

WITH ALMONDS AND GARBANZO BEANS

The jack o' lanterns are carved. The pumpkin seeds are toasting in the oven. Now what to do with all that pumpkin meat? The inspired answer is to make a casserole of pumpkin and garbanzo beans (chickpeas) and serve it in a hollowed-out pumpkin shell. This is the perfect dish for a Halloween potluck supper. Remember not to carve a face in the pumpkin you plan to use as a serving dish, and keep the little stemmed piece to use as a cover. If you're entertaining the whole block, you can double or triple the recipe and serve it in an extra-large pumpkin.

INGREDIENTS *Makes 4–6 servings*

2 tbsp olive oil

2 lbs pumpkin, or butternut squash, chopped

1 large leek, sliced

1 cup vegetable or chicken stock

1 16-oz bottle of tomato sauce

2 cups canned garbanzo beans

1 tbsp lemon juice

1 tbsp ground cumin

salt and black pepper

½ cup slivered almonds, toasted

1 cup natural/plain yogurt

2 tbsp fresh mint leaves, finely chopped

METHOD

1 Preheat oven to 350°F. Add the olive oil to a large flameproof casserole dish. Cook the pumpkin and leek over a moderate heat, stirring, until the leek is soft.

2 Add the stock, tomato sauce, garbanzo beans, lemon juice, and cumin, and season to taste with salt and pepper. Bring to a boil, then remove from the heat, and let cool very slightly.

3 Cover and bake in the oven for about 30 minutes or until the pumpkin is tender, stirring occasionally if necessary.

4 Remove from the oven. Stir in the toasted almonds. Combine the yogurt and mint and stir into the top of the casserole just before serving.

"He who sups well sleeps well."

MONDAY 25

AM · PM

TUESDAY 26

AM · PM

WEDNESDAY 27

AM · PM

THURSDAY 28

AM · PM

FRIDAY 29

AM · PM

QUICK TIP

Put your extra-virgin olive oil and balsamic vinegar in spray bottles to give you more control over the amount used. Spray skillets with oil before sautéing, or flavor a cooked chicken breast or fish fillet with a spritz of balsamic vinegar.

	Su	M	T	W	Th	F	S	Su	M	T	W	Th	F	S	Su	M	T	W	Th	F	S	Su	M	T	W	Th	F	S	Su	M	T	W	Th	F	S
SEPTEMBER						1	2	3	4	5	6	7	8	9	10	11	12	13	14	15	16	17	18	19	20	21	22	23	24	25	26	27	28	29	30
OCTOBER	1	2	3	4	5	6	7	8	9	10	11	12	13	14	15	16	17	18	19	20	21	22	23	24	25	26	27	28	29	30	31				
NOVEMBER		1	2	3	4	5	6	7	8	9	10	11	12	13	14	15	16	17	18	19	20	21	22	23	24	25	26	27	28	29	30				

COOK'S PANTRY

HARISSA PASTE

This fiery condiment is what gives North African cooking its kick. Put 2 oz dried chilies in a bowl and cover with hot water. Let stand for 2 hours. Drain the chilies and place in a food processor with 2 cloves garlic, 2 tablespoons olive oil, and a little salt. Process to a paste and then rub this through a fine sieve, being careful not to get any on your hands. Spoon into a clean screw-top jar, seal with a little oil before closing, and keep in the refrigerator for up to 3 months.

SATURDAY 30

SUNDAY 1   Yom Kippur begins at sundown

PANTRY RUNNING LOW ON

OCTOBER 2 – 8

"One cannot think well, love well, sleep well, if one has not dined well."

Virginia Woolf (1882–1941)

MONDAY 2

TUESDAY 3

WEDNESDAY 4

THURSDAY 5

FRIDAY 6

QUICK TIP

If you only need to add a little of any particular ingredient to a recipe, never pour straight into the bowl or pan. Always measure out into a spoon first so that you can't overdo it by mistake.

	Su	M	T	W	Th	F	S	Su	M	T	W	Th	F	S	Su	M	T	W	Th	F	S	Su	M	T	W	Th	F	S	Su	M	T	W	Th	F	S
SEPTEMBER						1	2	3	4	5	6	7	8	9	10	11	12	13	14	15	16	17	18	19	20	21	22	23	24	25	26	27	28	29	30
OCTOBER	1	2	3	4	5	6	7	8	9	10	11	12	13	14	15	16	17	18	19	20	21	22	23	24	25	26	27	28	29	30	31				
NOVEMBER		1	2	3	4	5	6	7	8	9	10	11	12	13	14	15	16	17	18	19	20	21	22	23	24	25	26	27	28	29	30				

FOOD IN A FLASH

THAI-STYLE BEEF WITH PEANUTS

(serves 2)

Heat 1 tablespoon peanut oil in a skillet. Add a 12-oz lean beef steak, and brown for 3–4 minutes on each side. Remove from the skillet and let the beef cool before shredding it into long strips. Return the skillet to the stove, add 1–2 tablespoons Asian chili paste and 3 fresh kaffir lime leaves, torn (optional), and cook for 1 minute. Add the beef and toss to coat. Combine ½ small romaine lettuce, ¼ cup chopped cilantro, ¼ cup chopped fresh mint, 1 tablespoon lime juice, and ½ tablespoon superfine sugar. Top this salad with the beef and sprinkle with chopped, roasted unsalted peanuts before serving.

SATURDAY 7

AM

PM

SUNDAY 8

AM

PM

PANTRY RUNNING LOW ON

"Enough is as good as a feast, and better than a surfeit."

MONDAY 9

Columbus Day,
Thanksgiving Day (Canada)

TUESDAY 10

WEDNESDAY 11

THURSDAY 12

FRIDAY 13

QUICK TIP

Use a pastry brush to coat an unbaked piecrust or flan shell with egg whites to "waterproof" it before adding a juicy filling, such as fruit. This will prevent the pastry from becoming too soggy.

	Su	M	T	W	Th	F	S	Su	M	T	W	Th	F	S	Su	M	T	W	Th	F	S	Su	M	T	W	Th	F	S	Su	M	T	W	Th	F	S
SEPTEMBER						1	2	3	4	5	6	7	8	9	10	11	12	13	14	15	16	17	18	19	20	21	22	23	24	25	26	27	28	29	30
OCTOBER	1	2	3	4	5	6	7	8	9	10	11	12	13	14	15	16	17	18	19	20	21	22	23	24	25	26	27	28	29	30	31
NOVEMBER		1	2	3	4	5	6	7	8	9	10	11	12	13	14	15	16	17	18	19	20	21	22	23	24	25	26	27	28	29	30

COOK'S PANTRY

PRESERVED LEMONS

Preserved lemons are used extensively in Middle Eastern and North African cooking. The peel is eaten, rather than the flesh, as it contains the essential flavor of the lemon. Wash 10 unwaxed lemons and cut each into 6–8 wedges. Press a generous amount of salt in the cut surfaces. Pack the wedges into two 2-pint sterilized jars. To each jar, add 2 tbsp salt and 6 tbsp lemon juice, then top up with boiling water. Cover and store in a cool, dark place for 2–4 weeks before using. They will keep for 1–2 years. To use, rinse thoroughly in cold water, discard the soft inner flesh, and thinly slice the rind as required.

SATURDAY 14

AM

PM

SUNDAY 15

AM

PM

PANTRY RUNNING LOW ON

OCTOBER 16 – 22

"One must ask children and birds how cherries and strawberries taste."

Johann Wolfgang von Goethe (1749–1832)

MONDAY 16

AM

PM

TUESDAY 17

AM

PM

WEDNESDAY 18

AM

PM

THURSDAY 19

AM

PM

FRIDAY 20

AM

PM

QUICK TIP

If you want to cut and serve really thin slices from a joint of cold meat you will find it much easier if you put the joint in the freezer for 30 minutes before you plan to carve it.

	Su	M	T	W	Th	F	S	Su	M	T	W	Th	F	S	Su	M	T	W	Th	F	S	Su	M	T	W	Th	F	S	Su	M	T	W	Th	F	S
SEPTEMBER						1	2	3	4	5	6	7	8	9	10	11	12	13	14	15	16	17	18	19	20	21	22	23	24	25	26	27	28	29	30
OCTOBER	1	2	3	4	5	6	7	8	9	10	11	12	13	14	15	16	17	18	19	20	21	22	23	24	25	26	27	28	29	30	31				
NOVEMBER		1	2	3	4	5	6	7	8	9	10	11	12	13	14	15	16	17	18	19	20	21	22	23	24	25	26	27	28	29	30				

FOOD IN A FLASH

QUICK CHILI CON CARNE
(serves 4)

Heat 1 tablespoon olive oil in a large saucepan and cook 1½ lbs lean ground beef until browned. Add ½ white onion, chopped, and 4 cloves garlic, crushed. Cook until the onion softens. Add ½ small bottle of beer, ½ cup beef stock, a 14-oz can crushed tomatoes, 2 tablespoons chili powder, 1 tablespoon ground cumin, 2–4 drops hot chili sauce (such as Tabasco), and a 14-oz can cooked kidney beans, and season to taste with salt and black pepper. Stir and bring to a boil, reduce the heat, and let simmer for 20–30 minutes until cooked. Sprinkle with chopped cilantro and serve with warmed flour tortillas.

SATURDAY 21

AM

PM

SUNDAY 22

AM

PM

PANTRY RUNNING LOW ON

OCTOBER 23 – 29

"Without lunch, what will become of love?"

Italian proverb

MONDAY 23

AM PM

TUESDAY 24

AM PM

WEDNESDAY 25

AM PM

THURSDAY 26

AM PM

FRIDAY 27

AM PM

QUICK TIP

Use the microwave to melt chocolate—it's by far the best way. Use a medium setting and check periodically, stirring occasionally. It's much better than a double boiler, which creates steam—a big no-no around chocolate.

	Su	M	T	W	Th	F	S	Su	M	T	W	Th	F	S	Su	M	T	W	Th	F	S	Su	M	T	W	Th	F	S	Su	M	T	W	Th	F	S
SEPTEMBER						1	2	3	4	5	6	7	8	9	10	11	12	13	14	15	16	17	18	19	20	21	22	23	24	25	26	27	28	29	30
OCTOBER	1	2	3	4	5	6	7	8	9	10	11	12	13	14	15	16	17	18	19	20	21	22	23	24	25	26	27	28	29	30	31				
NOVEMBER		1	2	3	4	5	6	7	8	9	10	11	12	13	14	15	16	17	18	19	20	21	22	23	24	25	26	27	28	29	30				

COOK'S PANTRY

MEXICAN-STYLE SPICED CHOCOLATE POWDER

Flavored with cinnamon, almonds, and vanilla, and having a grainier texture than other chocolates, Mexican chocolate is used in hot drinks and specialties such as *mole poblano*, the chili-almond sauce served with fowl. If you cannot buy Mexican chocolate you can make a good substitute. Simply break 4 oz bittersweet chocolate (minimum 70 per cent cocoa solids) into pieces and put it into a food processor. Add 2 teaspoons ground cinnamon and ¼ cup ground almonds. Process the ingredients to a fine powder, then tip into an airtight container and store in the refrigerator for up to 2 weeks.

SATURDAY 28

AM

PM

SUNDAY 29   Daylight Saving Time ends

AM

PM

PANTRY RUNNING LOW ON

Heirloom Potatoes

WITH GORGONZOLA, BABY SPINACH, AND PECAN NUTS

Every family has its traditional Thanksgiving dinner menu, often handed down through the generations. It can seem like heresy to depart from the old favorites. But whether you're hosting the meal or merely contributing a dish, why not slip something different in with the standards? Heirloom potatoes with spinach and Gorgonzola or blue cheese are a sophisticated alternative to the mashed potatoes on most holiday tables. (Check the farmers' market for heirloom varieties like La Ratte fingerlings or German butterballs.) This dish is so tasty that even the most determined traditionalist just might give it a permanent place among the family classics.

INGREDIENTS *Makes 6–8 servings*

2 lbs heirloom potatoes, unpeeled
½ cup pecan nuts, toasted and chopped

3 oz Gorgonzola or similar firm blue cheese, crumbled
¼ cup extra-virgin olive oil

2 cups baby spinach leaves, washed and stalks removed
salt and black pepper

METHOD

1 Wash the potatoes well and place them in a large saucepan. Add sufficient cold water to cover and salt generously.

2 Bring to a boil. Reduce the heat and simmer until the potatoes are just tender—how long this takes will depend on the variety.

3 When they are cooked, drain the potatoes in a colander and return to the warm pan. Using a wooden spoon, roughly crush the potatoes in the pot.

4 Add the pecans, Gorgonzola, and oil and stir to mix. Add the spinach and stir gently to blend. The spinach will wilt with the heat from the potatoes. Season to taste before transferring to a warmed serving dish.

"We should look for someone to eat and drink with before looking for something to eat and drink."

Epicurius (341–270BCE)

MONDAY 30

AM

PM

TUESDAY 31   Halloween

AM

PM

WEDNESDAY 1

AM

PM

THURSDAY 2

AM

PM

FRIDAY 3

AM

PM

QUICK TIP

To hold a large bowl in place when you are whisking, twist a kitchen towel into a rope, then form a circle with it. Place the bowl on top of the towel and it will stay in place.

	Su	M	T	W	Th	F	S	Su	M	T	W	Th	F	S	Su	M	T	W	Th	F	S	Su	M	T	W	Th	F	S	Su	M	T	W	Th	F	S	Su
OCTOBER	1	2	3	4	5	6	7	8	9	10	11	12	13	14	15	16	17	18	19	20	21	22	23	24	25	26	27	28	29	30	31
NOVEMBER					1	2	3	4	5	6	7	8	9	10	11	12	13	14	15	16	17	18	19	20	21	22	23	24	25	26	27	28	29	30
DECEMBER		1	2	3	4	5	6	7	8	9	10	11	12	13	14	15	16	17	18	19	20	21	22	23	24	25	26	27	28	29	30	31

FOOD IN A FLASH

PEAR AND ALMOND GALETTES
(serves 2)

Preheat the oven to 350°F. Cut 5 oz defrosted readymade puff pastry into 2 pieces of equal size. Roll each one out into a rectangle on a floured counter until the longest edge is at least 6 inches long. Sprinkle 1 tablespoon ground almonds over each, top with thin slices of peeled and cored pear, leaving a border around the edge. Brush with melted butter and sprinkle with Demerara sugar. Bake for 20 minutes or until golden. Serve warm with a scoop of good-quality vanilla ice cream.

SATURDAY 4

AM

PM

SUNDAY 5

AM

PM

PANTRY RUNNING LOW ON

NOVEMBER 6 – 12

"Hunger is the spice of food."

MONDAY 6

AM

PM

TUESDAY 7

AM

PM

WEDNESDAY 8

AM

PM

THURSDAY 9

AM

PM

FRIDAY 10

AM

PM

QUICK TIP

The best way to peel fresh ginger root is by using a dinner spoon. Simply scrape the tip of the spoon across the surface of the ginger. It's easy, fast, and makes little waste.

	Su	M	T	W	Th	F	S	Su	M	T	W	Th	F	S	Su	M	T	W	Th	F	S	Su	M	T	W	Th	F	S	Su	M	T	W	Th	F	S	Su
OCTOBER		1	2	3	4	5	6	7	8	9	10	11	12	13	14	15	16	17	18	19	20	21	22	23	24	25	26	27	28	29	30	31
NOVEMBER			1	2	3	4	5	6	7	8	9	10	11	12	13	14	15	16	17	18	19	20	21	22	23	24	25	26	27	28	29	30
DECEMBER			1	2	3	4	5	6	7	8	9	10	11	12	13	14	15	16	17	18	19	20	21	22	23	24	25	26	27	28	29	30	31

COOK'S PANTRY

FRESH GINGER IN A JAR

Fresh ginger is extremely popular in a wide variety
of Asian stir-fry and curry dishes. If you like to cook
Oriental dishes, it's a good idea to keep supplies
of ready-grated ginger root on hand. Peel the skin
off a piece of fresh root ginger. Grate the ginger,
taking care not to graze your fingers. Put it in an
airtight jar, add a small amount of sherry and it
will keep in the refrigerator for several weeks.

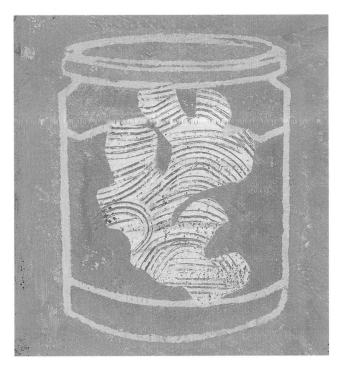

SATURDAY 11   Veterans' Day
Remembrance Day (Canada)

AM

PM

SUNDAY 12

AM

PM

PANTRY RUNNING LOW ON

"It's good food and not fine words that keep me alive."

Molière (1622–1673)

MONDAY 13

AM

PM

TUESDAY 14

AM

PM

WEDNESDAY 15

AM

PM

THURSDAY 16

AM

PM

FRIDAY 17

AM

PM

QUICK TIP

Cut a deep cross into the leaf end of scallions and leave them to soak in ice water in the refrigerator. They will open like flowers and can be used as a garnish in soups or with rice and noodle dishes.

	Su	M	T	W	Th	F	S	Su	M	T	W	Th	F	S	Su	M	T	W	Th	F	S	Su	M	T	W	Th	F	S	Su	M	T	W	Th	F	S	Su
OCTOBER		1	2	3	4	5	6	7	8	9	10	11	12	13	14	15	16	17	18	19	20	21	22	23	24	25	26	27	28	29	30	31
NOVEMBER			1	2	3	4	5	6	7	8	9	10	11	12	13	14	15	16	17	18	19	20	21	22	23	24	25	26	27	28	29	30
DECEMBER			1	2	3	4	5	6	7	8	9	10	11	12	13	14	15	16	17	18	19	20	21	22	23	24	25	26	27	28	29	30	31

FOOD IN A FLASH

GREEN BEANS WITH CRISPY FRIED CHILI AND GARLIC

(serves 2)

Place ½ lb green French beans, trimmed, in a steamer over boiling water to cook until tender. Place 2 teaspoons sesame oil in a hot wok or skillet with 1–2 large red chilies, chopped, 1 garlic clove, sliced, ¼ teaspoon sea salt, and ¼ teaspoon cracked black pepper. Cook for 2 minutes, then toss with the green beans. Serve immediately as a side dish.

SATURDAY 18

SUNDAY 19

PANTRY RUNNING LOW ON

NOVEMBER 20 – 26

"Diet cures more than the lancet."

MONDAY 20

AM

PM

TUESDAY 21

AM

PM

WEDNESDAY 22

AM

PM

THURSDAY 23 Thanksgiving Day (US)

AM

PM

FRIDAY 24

AM

PM

QUICK TIP

If you add chopped garlic to a long-simmering dish at the beginning of the cooking process it will lose most of its nutrients by the time it reaches the table. Instead, pound the garlic to a paste with a little olive oil and salt, and stir into the dish just before serving.

	Su	M	T	W	Th	F	S	Su	M	T	W	Th	F	S	Su	M	T	W	Th	F	S	Su	M	T	W	Th	F	S	Su	M	T	W	Th	F	S	Su
OCTOBER		1	2	3	4	5	6	7	8	9	10	11	12	13	14	15	16	17	18	19	20	21	22	23	24	25	26	27	28	29	30	31
NOVEMBER			1	2	3	4	5	6	7	8	9	10	11	12	13	14	15	16	17	18	19	20	21	22	23	24	25	26	27	28	29	30
DECEMBER			1	2	3	4	5	6	7	8	9	10	11	12	13	14	15	16	17	18	19	20	21	22	23	24	25	26	27	28	29	30	31

COOK'S PANTRY

CLARIFIED BUTTER

Clarified butter or *ghee* is widely used in Indian cooking, particularly for frying spices at the beginning of recipes. Because it contains no milk solids, it can be heated to a higher temperature than ordinary butter and is excellent for butter sauces and fried dishes. To make, simply melt two sticks of butter in a saucepan over a low heat. Skim off the frothy milk solids that rise to the top, then pour the layer of golden liquid into a clean bowl, and chill.

SATURDAY 25

SUNDAY 26

PANTRY RUNNING LOW ON

Roast Cornish Game Hens

WITH CRANBERRY GLAZE AND SWEET POTATO MASH

This month, many holidays converge. From Christmas to Hanukkah to Kwanzaa to New Year's Eve, celebratory feasts abound. You can always serve the traditional fare, usually a stuffed turkey or a roast. But what to do with the leftovers? Confronted with the third night of turkey hash, the best cook is ready to throw in the towel. Cornish game hens to the rescue. What an elegant bird for a holiday meal. Even the name is romantic. Best of all, no leftovers.

INGREDIENTS *Makes 4 servings*

2 large sweet potatoes (12 to 14-oz each), unpeeled

2 tbsp (¼ stick) unsalted butter

2 tbsp fresh orange juice

1 tsp finely grated fresh orange zest

a pinch of nutmeg

salt and black pepper

1 cup sugar

1 cup water

1 cup fresh cranberries

¼ cup ruby port

2 Cornish game hens, halved lengthwise

METHOD

1 Preheat oven to 425°F. Prick the potatoes and bake on a baking sheet in the middle of the oven until tender—about 1¼ hours. When cool enough to handle, remove skins and discard. Transfer to a large bowl, add the butter, orange juice and zest, and nutmeg, and mash together. Season to taste.

2 Meanwhile bring the sugar, water, cranberries, and port to simmer in a heavy saucepan over medium-high heat, stirring until the sugar dissolves. Boil until reduced to 1 cup, stirring frequently for about 20 minutes. Purée in a processor and return to a small saucepan. Set aside.

3 Reduce oven to 400°F. Place the game hens, cut side down, on a baking sheet. Season well. Bake for 30 minutes, and then increase the oven temperature to 450°F. Continue baking until the juices run clear when the thickest part of the thigh is pierced—about 20 minutes longer.

4 Reheat the potato mash and sauce, and serve alongside the roasted hens.

"The proof of the pudding is in the eating."

MONDAY 27

AM

PM

TUESDAY 28

AM

PM

WEDNESDAY 29

AM

PM

THURSDAY 30

AM

PM

FRIDAY 1

AM

PM

QUICK TIP

Excess grease in casseroles and stock pots can be easily removed by throwing in a few ice cubes. Before they melt the fat will stick to them and you can then scoop them out with a slotted spoon.

	Su	M	T	W	Th	F	S	Su	M	T	W	Th	F	S	Su	M	T	W	Th	F	S	Su	M	T	W	Th	F	S	Su	M	T	W	Th	F	S	Su
NOVEMBER		1	2	3	4	5	6	7	8	9	10	11	12	13	14	15	16	17	18	19	20	21	22	23	24	25	26	**27**	**28**	**29**	**30**
DECEMBER							1	2	3	4	5	6	7	8	9	10	11	12	13	14	15	16	17	18	19	20	21	22	23	24	25	26	27	28	29	30	31
JANUARY		1	2	3	4	5	6	7	8	9	10	11	12	13	14	15	16	17	18	19	20	21	22	23	24	25	26	27	28	29	30	31

FOOD IN A FLASH

COUNTRY-STYLE SAUSAGE AND LENTIL CASSEROLE
(serves 2)

Broil or barbecue 4 sausages until browned all over and cooked through. Meanwhile, heat 1 tablespoon olive oil in a saucepan, add ½ medium brown onion, finely chopped, and 1 clove garlic, crushed. Cook, stirring, until the onion softens. Add 1 celery stalk, trimmed and finely chopped, 1 medium zucchini, sliced, and 2 slices bacon, chopped. Cook, stirring, until the celery softens. Add ¼ cup chicken stock, 1 cup canned crushed tomatoes, and 1 tablespoon tomato paste, and bring to a boil. Add 7 oz cooked or canned brown lentils and heat through. Spoon the lentil sauce over the sausages and sprinkle with chopped fresh thyme before serving.

SATURDAY 2

AM

PM

SUNDAY 3

AM

PM

PANTRY RUNNING LOW ON

DECEMBER 4 – 10

"Good seed makes a good crop."

MONDAY 4

AM

PM

TUESDAY 5

AM

PM

WEDNESDAY 6

AM

PM

THURSDAY 7

AM

PM

FRIDAY 8

AM

PM

QUICK TIP

No matter what kind of baking sheet you're using, line it with parchment paper and your cookies won't burn on the bottom. Bake tarts on a pizza stone—it makes a big difference in getting the bottoms to cook.

	Su	M	T	W	Th	F	S	Su	M	T	W	Th	F	S	Su	M	T	W	Th	F	S	Su	M	T	W	Th	F	S	Su	M	T	W	Th	F	S	Su
NOVEMBER		1	2	3	4	5	6	7	8	9	10	11	12	13	14	15	16	17	18	19	20	21	22	23	24	25	26	27	28	29	30				
DECEMBER			1	2	3	4	5	6	7	8	9	10	11	12	13	14	15	16	17	18	19	20	21	22	23	24	25	26	27	28	29	30	31		
JANUARY	1	2	3	4	5	6	7	8	9	10	11	12	13	14	15	16	17	18	19	20	21	22	23	24	25	26	27	28	29	30	31					

COOK'S PANTRY

NUT BUTTERS

These are truly delicious and very easy to make at home. This offers the added advantage of knowing that they do not contain additives or excessive amounts of sugar. Place ¾ cup shelled nuts of your choice (such as peanuts, cashews, almonds, or hazelnuts) in a food processor and process until they are finely and evenly ground. Pour 1–2 tablespoons sunflower oil into the processor and blend again to achieve a coarse paste. Store in a clean, airtight jar, and in a cool, dark place. Nut butters will keep for 2–3 months.

SATURDAY 9

AM

PM

SUNDAY 10

AM

PM

PANTRY RUNNING LOW ON

"A man cannot have a pure mind who refuses apple-dumplings."
Charles Lamb (1775–1834)

MONDAY 11

AM

PM

TUESDAY 12

AM

PM

WEDNESDAY 13

AM

PM

THURSDAY 14

AM

PM

FRIDAY 15   Hanukkah begins at sundown

AM

PM

QUICK TIP

Eggplants absorb large quantities of oil during frying. Salting helps to reduce this. Cut the eggplant into slices, place in a strainer, and sprinkle generously with salt. Let stand for about one hour, then rinse well and pat dry with kitchen paper before frying.

	Su	M	T	W	Th	F	S	Su	M	T	W	Th	F	S	Su	M	T	W	Th	F	S	Su	M	T	W	Th	F	S	Su	M	T	W	Th	F	S	Su
NOVEMBER		1	2	3	4	5	6	7	8	9	10	11	12	13	14	15	16	17	18	19	20	21	22	23	24	25	26	27	28	29	30				
DECEMBER			1	2	3	4	5	6	7	8	9	10	11	12	13	14	15	16	17	18	19	20	21	22	23	24	25	26	27	28	29	30	31		
JANUARY	1	2	3	4	5	6	7	8	9	10	11	12	13	14	15	16	17	18	19	20	21	22	23	24	25	26	27	28	29	30	31				

FOOD IN A FLASH

SPICED EGGPLANT CURRY
(serves 2)

Heat 2 tablespoons groundnut oil in a skillet and fry
1 medium onion, chopped, until soft. Add 1 green chili
pepper, chopped, and 1 large eggplant, cut into 1-inch
cubes. Cook for 5 minutes over a medium heat. Add 2
tomatoes, seeded and roughly chopped, and stir in ¾ cup
vegetable stock. Cook for 15 minutes until the eggplant is
soft. Add 1 teaspoon garam masala (Indian spice blend,
optional), ¼ cup chopped fresh cilantro, and season to taste
with salt and black pepper. Stir in ¼ cup plain yogurt just
before serving with a warm Indian flat bread, such as naan.

SATURDAY 16

AM

PM

SUNDAY 17

AM

PM

PANTRY RUNNING LOW ON

"The company makes the feast."

MONDAY 18

AM

PM

TUESDAY 19

AM

PM

WEDNESDAY 20

AM

PM

THURSDAY 21

AM

PM

FRIDAY 22   First Day of Winter

AM

PM

QUICK TIP

Thicken a too-runny sauce by mixing a little cornstarch with water, adding the paste to your sauce, and letting it to cook through. Pass a curdled sauce through a sieve to remove lumps.

	Su	M	T	W	Th	F	S	Su	M	T	W	Th	F	S	Su	M	T	W	Th	F	S	Su	M	T	W	Th	F	S	Su	M	T	W	Th	F	S	Su
NOVEMBER		1	2	3	4	5	6	7	8	9	10	11	12	13	14	15	16	17	18	19	20	21	22	23	24	25	26	27	28	29	30
DECEMBER			1	2	3	4	5	6	7	8	9	10	11	12	13	14	15	16	17	18	19	20	21	22	23	24	25	26	27	28	29	30	31
JANUARY	1	2	3	4	5	6	7	8	9	10	11	12	13	14	15	16	17	18	19	20	21	22	23	24	25	26	27	28	29	30	31

COOK'S PANTRY

MIXED (OR PUDDING) SPICE

This English blend of spices is traditionally used to flavor steamed puddings and apple cakes but it will give a nice lift to any baked goods containing dried fruit, including muffins. Use a pestle and mortar to grind together 1 tablespoon cilantro seeds, a 2-inch cinnamon stick, 1 teaspoon allspice berries, and 1 teaspoon cloves. Stir in 1 tablespoon grated nutmeg and 2 teaspoons ground ginger. Store in an airtight container and use in small quantities.

SATURDAY 23

A M

P M

SUNDAY 24

A M

P M

PANTRY RUNNING LOW ON

"The discovery of a new dish does more for the happiness of mankind than the discovery of a star."

Anthelme Brillat-Savarin (1755–1826)

MONDAY 25 | Christmas Day

AM

PM

TUESDAY 26 | Boxing Day (Canada), Kwanzaa begins

AM

PM

WEDNESDAY 27

AM

PM

THURSDAY 28

AM

PM

FRIDAY 29

AM

PM

QUICK TIP

Any chocolate will quickly absorb both moisture and odors from the air. To keep it tasting good it's best to always store it in plastic wrap or in an airtight container away from herbs, spices, or other aromatics.

	Su	M	T	W	Th	F	S	Su	M	T	W	Th	F	S	Su	M	T	W	Th	F	S	Su	M	T	W	Th	F	S	Su	M	T	W	Th	F	S	Su
NOVEMBER		1	2	3	4	5	6	7	8	9	10	11	12	13	14	15	16	17	18	19	20	21	22	23	24	25	26	27	28	29	30				
DECEMBER			1	2	3	4	5	6	7	8	9	10	11	12	13	14	15	16	17	18	19	20	21	22	23	24	25	26	27	28	29	30	31		
JANUARY	1	2	3	4	5	6	7	8	9	10	11	12	13	14	15	16	17	18	19	20	21	22	23	24	25	26	27	28	29	30	31				

FOOD IN A FLASH

WARM CHOCOLATE FONDUE
(serves 4–6)
Place 1¼ cups water, 1½ cups granulated sugar, and 1½ cups corn syrup into a saucepan and bring to a boil. Simmer for 10–15 minutes until the sugar solution has reduced slightly. Remove from the heat, add 1 cup sifted premium cocoa powder, and whisk until smooth. Return the pan to the stove, add ½ cup plus 5 tablespoons heavy cream, bring to a boil, and allow to simmer for 5 minutes. Remove from the heat and stir in 5 oz semisweet chocolate, chopped. Pour into a fondue pot and keep warm. Serve with pieces of fresh fruit and marshmallows for dunking.

SATURDAY 30

AM

PM

SUNDAY 31   New Year's Eve

AM

PM

PANTRY RUNNING LOW ON

WEIGHT

½ oz	15 g
1 oz	25 g
2 oz	55 g
3½ oz	100 g
4 oz	115 g
5½ oz	150 g
6 oz	175 g
7 oz	200 g
8 oz	225 g
9 oz	250 g
12 oz	350 g
1 lb	450 g
1 lb 2 oz	500 g
2 lb 4 oz	1 kg

VOLUME

¼ tsp	1.25 ml
½ tsp	2.5 ml
1 tsp	5 ml
1 tbsp	15 ml
1 fl oz	30 ml
2 fl oz	60 ml
3 fl oz	75 ml
3½ fl oz	100 ml
4 fl oz (¼ pint)	120 ml
8 fl oz (½ pint)	240 ml
1 pint	480 ml
1½ pints	720 ml
2 pints	960 ml
2 pints 1 fl oz	1 liter

CUP MEASUREMENTS

Rice (uncooked)	1 cup	7 oz	200 g
Potatoes (peeled and diced)	1 cup	6 oz	175 g
Potatoes (mashed)	1 cup	8 oz	225 g
Onions (chopped)	1 cup	4 oz	115 g
Tomatoes	1 cup	8 oz	225 g
Meat (minced)	1 cup (packed)	8 oz	225 g
Fish (cooked and flaked)	1 cup (packed)	8 oz	225 g
Shrimp (peeled)	1 cup	6 oz	175 g
Nuts (chopped)	1 cup	4 oz	115 g
Grated cheese	1 cup	4 oz	115 g
Cream cheese	1 cup	8 oz	225 g
Butter	1 cup	8 oz	225 g
Butter	1 stick	8 tbsp	100 g
Flour	1 cup	4 oz	115 g
Golden syrup, treacle	1 cup	12 oz	350 g
Currants, sultanas	1 cup	5½ oz	150 g

Note: Be sure to stick with either imperial or metric measurements when cooking—never mix the two within one recipe. Most conversions are not exact and you could well spoil the recipe.

Family mealtimes today tend to be relaxed affairs but there are some occasions when a more formal table setting is appropriate. Laying an elegant table need not be daunting. It's best to stick to an uncluttered arrangement and to follow the popular convention of placing the utensil to be used first on the outside. As host your primary concern should be that your guests feel comfortable and not intimidated. Sparkling glassware, china, and cutlery are essential and starched linen napkins will add a special touch.

International informal

This is the most popular setting. The dinner knife is placed to the right of the dinner plate, with the blade facing the plate, and the soup spoon sits to the right of the knife. The dinner fork sits to the left of the plate, with the napkin neatly folded and laid here too. The dessert fork and spoon are laid horizontally above the plate, the fork first and with the handle facing left and the spoon above it with the handle to the right. Both a glass for red wine and a glass for white wine should be provided, along with a water glass.

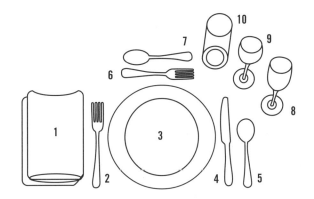

1 Napkin in a simple fold   2 Dinner fork   3 Dinner plate
4 Dinner knife   5 Soup spoon   6 Dessert fork   7 Dessert spoon
8 White wine glass   9 Red wine glass   10 Water glass

American formal

This classic setting is for a three-course meal with either a fish or a salad entrée (include either fish or salad cutlery as appropriate). The dinner knife is placed to the right of the dinner plate, with the fish knife (if needed) to its right. The dinner fork sits to the left of the plate, with the fish knife and/or salad fork to its left, and the napkin neatly folded and placed here too. The dessert fork and spoon are placed horizontally above the plate, the fork first and with the handle facing left and the spoon above it with the handle to the right. (It is not necessary to provide both if the dessert does not require them.) A butter knife is optional and should be laid on the bread and butter plate. Both a red and a white wine glass should be provided, along with a water glass.

1 Napkin in a simple fold   2 Salad fork   3 Fish fork   4 Dinner fork
5 Dinner plate   6 Dinner knife   7 Fish knife   8 Dessert fork
9 Dessert spoon   10 White wine glass   11 Red wine glass
12 Water glass   13 Bread and butter plate

SERVING COCKTAILS AT HOME

If you wish to make and serve good cocktails at home it's worth investing in a few accessories that will help you "mix" with style. The most important piece of bar equipment is a spirit measure or jigger. Cocktails should be a precise blend of ingredients and too much of one element can spoil the end result. The modern dual-measure, featuring a cup for both single (1 oz) and double (2 oz) measures, is ideal. The cocktail shaker is the second most important tool. Choose a standard 3-piece stainless steel shaker, with a beaker, a lid with a built-in strainer, and a twist-off cap. Other useful pieces of equipment include a long-handled bar spoon, especially useful for stirring tall drinks; a muddler (resembling a small wooden pestle), for mashing or crushing ingredients such as fruit, herbs, or sugar cubes; an ice bucket with tongs and an ice-crushing machine; a sharp kitchen knife; and a citrus press. Finally, cocktail glasses are essential for polished presentation and choosing the right one for each drink is crucial. There are six basic shapes:

Martini or Cocktail
This thin-stemmed, wide-necked glass is probably the one most identified with cocktails. It is designed to keep the warmth of your hand away from the drink.

Old-fashioned or Rocks
This is a squat, straight-sided glass with a heavy base that is most often used to serve whiskey or bourbon on the rocks. It should be used when making any drink that contains muddled fruit or herbs as the sturdy base will withstand the muddling process.

Highball or Collins
This is a tall, straight-sided glass used for long drinks that require plenty of ice.

Margarita or Coupette
Similar to the Martini glass in shape but sturdier, the Margarita or Coupette glass has a wide rim that makes it perfect for salting.

Champagne flute
It's hard to beat the elegance of a long-stemmed and narrow-rimmed Champagne flute. It is perfect for any Champagne cocktail as the shape of the bowl retains the maximum amount of bubbles.

Wine glass
Although not specifically designed for serving cocktails, a large wine glass can work well for many drinks. It makes a good all-rounder and alternative to the more specialist glassware.

To hone your cocktail-making skills why not try the following recipes and enjoy sampling a different cocktail each month of the year.

JANUARY

Bloody Mary

A savory cocktail with a spicy kick, perfect for serving at a weekend brunch party.

1½ oz vodka
3 oz tomato juice
1 oz lemon juice
1 teaspoon Worcestershire sauce
2 drops Tabasco (optional)
Salt and pepper
Slice of lemon

Put a few cubes of ice in a shaker and add the liquid ingredients. Shake well and then strain into an Old-fashioned glass. Season to taste with salt and pepper and decorate with a slice of lemon.

FEBRUARY

Chocolate Martini

Opulent, indulgent, and the perfect way to spoil a loved one on Valentine's Day.

2 oz vodka
½ oz crème de cacao (or similar chocolate liqueur)
Chocolate vermicelli to garnish

Put a few cubes of ice in a shaker and add the liquid ingredients. Stir and pour into a Martini glass. Decorate the top with a sprinkle of chocolate vermicelli.

MARCH

Black Velvet

A simply delicious Gaelic drink, perfect for celebrating St. Patrick's Day in style.

½ Highball glass chilled bitter stout (such as Guinness)
½ Highball glass chilled Champagne or good-quality sparkling dry white wine

Simply pour the stout into a highball glass, tipping the glass as you pour to avoid a frothy head, and top up with the Champagne.

APRIL

Caipirinha

A fresh and zesty drink that's a beautiful vivid green, just perfect for Spring!

1 lime (cut into eighths)
2 teaspoon brown sugar
2 oz cachaca (Brazilian sugar-cane rum)
1 cup crushed ice

Muddle the lime together with the sugar in an Old-fashioned glass. Fill the glass with crushed ice. Pour in the cachaca and stir. Top with more crushed ice. Serve with two short straws.

MAY

Mint Julep

The traditional drink of the Kentucky Derby, May is the month to kick back and enjoy this Southern classic.

A handful of fresh mint leaves
1 tsp superfine sugar
a swoosh of soda
2–3 oz bourbon
crushed ice to serve

Frost a Highball glass in the refrigerator before you start. Muddle the mint leaves and the sugar in the bottom of an Old-fashioned glass and add a small swoosh of soda. Transfer the mixture to the frosted Highball, pack the glass with crushed ice, and pour over the bourbon. Stir gently until the sugar is completely dissolved. Serve with long straws.

JUNE

Social Climber

A pretty and fresh drink, the perfect aperitif for a summer lunch.

2 oz vodka (raspberry-flavored if available)
½ oz crème de cassis
½ oz fresh lime juice
a few fresh raspberries

Put a few cubes of ice in a shaker and add the liquid ingredients. Shake and strain into a chilled Martini glass. Decorate with the raspberries.

JULY

Independence Day Punch

What do you serve at your July 4th barbecue? This—it's perfect for large gatherings and very simple to prepare. (Makes 30 cups.)

1 bottle chilled Champagne or good sparkling white wine
1 bottle cognac
3 bottles dry red wine
1 pint strong tea
juice of 2 dozen lemons
2 lb superfine sugar
lemon slices to garnish

In a large punch bowl dissolve the sugar in the lemon juice. Add the tea, and some large chunks of ice, then the wine and cognac. Chill thoroughly. Immediately before serving, pour in the Champagne. Serve in wine glasses and decorate with lemon slices.

AUGUST

Frozen Margarita

There is only one cocktail that really hits the spot in the heat of the summer—it's the Mexican classic, the margarita.

3 oz tequila
1 oz Cointreau
a wedge of lime

2–3 oz fresh lime juice
crushed ice
saucer dusted with coarse salt

Take a Margarita or Martini glass and moisten the edge with the lime wedge. Upturn the glass into the salt to coat the rim. Put the tequila, Cointreau, lime juice, and ice into a blender. Blend until smooth. Serve garnished with the wedge of lime.

SEPTEMBER

Cosmopolitan

It's the end of summer and, for some people, time to return to the city. Soften the blow with the most sophisticated of all cocktails.

2 fl oz vodka (lemon if available)
1 fl oz triple sec
2 oz cranberry juice
dash of lime juice

Put a few cubes of ice into a cocktail shaker and add all of the ingredients. Shake well and strain into a Martini glass.

OCTOBER

Rusty Nail

A warm, spicy after-dinner drink, perfect for Fall evenings when you fancy something a little more interesting than plain whiskey.

2 fl oz whiskey
1 fl oz Drambuie
a twist of lemon

Pour the whiskey straight into an Old-fashioned glass, add the Drambuie, and stir. Decorate with a twist of lemon placed in the drink. Note: a "twist" of lemon is a thin, curled, pared-off slice of the peel.

NOVEMBER

Thanksgiving Cocktail

An excellent way to whet your appetite for the traditional turkey feast.

1 oz dry gin
1 oz dry vermouth
1 oz apricot brandy
a few drops of lemon juice
1 maraschino cherry

Put a few cubes of ice into a cocktail shaker and add the liquid ingredients. Shake and strain into Martini glass. Garnish with a maraschino cherry.

DECEMBER

Winter Mule

A delicate, wintry cocktail, guaranteed to warm up the coldest of days.

2 oz stem ginger syrup
2 oz white rum
juice of a fresh lime
crushed ice to serve

Put a few cubes of ice in a shaker and add the liquid ingredients. Shake well and strain into a Champagne flute filled with crushed ice. Garnish with a slice of fresh lime.

COOK'S NOTES

COOK'S NOTES